T0208617

OFF LIMITS

this struggle will not overtake me

Onesimus Williams

authorHOUSE®

AuthorHouse™
1663 Liberty Drive
Bloomington, IN 47403
www.authorhouse.com
Phone: 1 (800) 839-8640

Onesimus Williams
P.O. Box 2272
Smyrna, Georgia 30081

Scripture quotations marked KJV are from the Holy Bible,
King James Version (Authorized Version). First published
in 1611. Quoted from the KJV Classic Reference Bible,
Copyright © 1983 by The Zondervan Corporation.

Published by AuthorHouse 03/20/2015

ISBN: 978-1-4969-7128-9 (sc)
ISBN: 978-1-4969-7127-2 (e)

Library of Congress Control Number: 2015902845

Print information available on the last page.

Manuscript editing by Roslyn L. Thomas

This book is printed on acid-free paper.

All references to satan or devil have been lower
cased on purpose throughout this book.

Contents

Dedication

I would like to dedicate this book to one of my best friends, Demario Tucker. He has truly been like an older brother to me; always consistent and full of character and integrity. Individuals of his caliber are such a rarity in today's society. Thank you for always being my brother!

To my wonderful mother, the one and only, Minister Janet Greene. Thanks for all of the many sacrifices that you've made to be sure I would become all that God has called me to be. The older I become, I realize that there are a lot of parents that choose not to sacrifice for their children. One thing I do know is that if no one else in the world is praying for me, I KNOW Janet has got me covered. Thanks Mom!

Introduction

This book was written primarily to born-again believers; however, you can definitely take these tools and principles to witness or minister to anyone dealing with sexual issues. The first step in deliverance is salvation because without the power of the blood of Jesus your fight is in vain.

Of all the books that I could write about, you might ask, "What inspired you to write about getting free from sexual struggles?" This material emerged from my growing concern for men in the Body of Christ who were seeking freedom but had nowhere to go for help. The Christian community is a wonderful environment when we follow the Word, but it can also be one of the most critical and judgmental places to go when we're hurting. I didn't write this book because I wanted to be famous or make money. I saw how so many men were living in bondage and weren't free and it disturbed my spirit. Many men are coming to church week after week and still living in a spiritual prison. They feel like no one understands their struggle or is willing to admit that they deal with the same thing.

The reasons that qualify me to write on such a robust subject:

- I have been born-again and filled with the Spirit (25 years) long enough to know what I'm talking about, give accurate doctrine, and hear from the Spirit of God what He wants to share with His people.

- I have ministered to men through small group settings along these lines since 2002.

- I am a virgin and will continue to live celibate until marriage. So, I can definitely tell you how to stay free, keep your mind right, and keep your flesh under.

- Most importantly, I am a man just like you, and I'm not afraid to tell you the truth.

You may think that you've read a men's book like this one before but I promise you have never read anything more real or transparent than this. I want to prepare you now that this book is for men who are serious and want to get beyond repenting every week about the same old thing. I will give you practical steps, confessions, scriptures, and prayers to pray. It's time to put on your big boy underwear, and let's get free and *STAY FREE*!

As you continue to read this book, I am confident in the Greater One who inspired me to write it that your life will be transformed forever. This evil spirit that has bound you for so long will be broken. John 8:32 says, "And ye shall know the truth, and the truth shall make you free."

Identify

Chapter 1

What Snares You?

I want to begin with what may seem obvious to some but very few have taken the time to recognize the effects of what snares them. We, as Christian men, have not been completely honest with ourselves and consequently we have been trapped without knowing the reason. We have not been told that our desires are real; therefore, we try to ignore the very thing that catches our attention. You must come to a point of honesty in what your flesh is calling out to get. You might ask, "Why is this important to identify?" It's important because the first clause of James 1:14 tells us that "...every man is tempted..." What causes this temptation? This verse further reveals that temptation comes from your own lust, which is something you desire.

> "But every man is tempted, when he is drawn away of his own lust, and enticed." James 1:14

Now that we have established that truth let's talk about how the enemy comes in to pervert desires. For example, you have identified that you like a woman that has long, curly hair with an hour glass shape. The enemy will take this information and present it to you outside of the boundaries of the Word of God. Instead of only getting you to acknowledge her beauty, the enemy presents this elaborate scenario that is lustful and sexual in nature to entice you. Something within your flesh desired sexual fulfillment, and he introduced the thought of it being with her. The same is true with men that deal with same-sex attractions. Something in your flesh desires sexual fulfillment with another man. We know these desires are not godly according to the Word of God; however, you cannot negate that they do exist.

You cannot address what you don't acknowledge! Facts are real, feelings are real, and lust is real. I cannot tell you how many times I have heard men say when they are tempted, "Well, I just try to get my mind off of the temptation or find something else to do." You are only avoiding the issue hoping that it will go away, but if you don't address it, it will return. Notice James 4:7 told us to "... Resist the devil, and he will flee from you." It didn't say ignore the devil or act like he's not there, it said "resist." In Chapter 16 we will talk more about how to resist the devil and plead the blood of Jesus.

If you don't understand that the desire of your flesh is the bait that the enemy will use against you, you will fall subject to it every single time. The scripture I referenced earlier, James 1:14, used an interesting phrase, "drawn away." How does this happen? satan is very studious when it comes to finding weaknesses in men. He is not omniscient (all-knowing), but he is very watchful. Since you were a little boy, the enemy has been sending bait your way to see which one would catch your attention the most. Sexual desire is not evil but was created to be expressed within the confines of marriage. When you allow your flesh to take this outside of the marriage covenant, you are opening up your soul (mind, will and emotions) for the enemy to set up shop in your life.

The enemy really doesn't have many tricks. I can almost guarantee you that he comes to you with the same temptation every time. It may come in different forms or styles, but it's the same trap because he has identified what appeals to your flesh. I'll prove it to you. How many times have you told yourself,

"I promise, I'm only going to do this one more time and then I'm not fooling with this anymore?" Let me answer that question for you...hundreds. You probably can't even count or dare to remember. As you arm yourself with the Word of God, your spirit will grow stronger and more alert, and it will become very easy to identify the devil and stop him in his tracks.

Temptation Triggers

There are certain situations in life that can trigger a response from you. According to Dictionary.com, a trigger is defined as "anything, as an act or event that serves as a stimulus and initiates or precipitates a reaction or series of reactions."[1]

"Lest satan should get an advantage of us: for we are not ignorant of his devices." II Corinthians 2:11

This scripture admonishes us that we should not be ignorant of the devices of the enemy. A device is designed to set something in motion or to turn something on for a particular task. Take for instance a remote control, what does that device do? If you press the power button on the remote it will turn on the television. If you turn on your iPod, select a song and press play, music will come on. Most devices have a power button to turn the device on and off, and additional buttons are there for the different functions of the device.

The reason why most men get into trouble is because they have not identified the triggers of life. Sexual temptation is not the trigger. It is simply one of the buttons that satan will use on the menu list. The trigger is represented by the power button. Before you can switch to a channel or select something different, you must first turn on the power. What triggers you? There are so many triggers in life which can include stress, discouragement, busyness, pressure, failure, loneliness, etc., and for each guy the trigger is something different.

Have you noticed how easy it is to accept satan's "menu items" (i.e. sex, pornography, masturbation, etc.) during times of trouble when your trigger has been initiated? Why? It's because your defenses are down, and during these times your spirit is not as alert as it should be. The interesting thing about triggers is that they will initiate something, whether good or bad. You must identify what you have conditioned your triggers to initiate.

I know a trigger for me is being overwhelmed. When I become overwhelmed, I know it's time for me to step away from what I am doing and relax. Unfortunately, most men ignore the triggers and keep pressing through them not realizing that they will eventually break under pressure. We were not designed to be under intense pressure for extended periods of time. This is how little weights become addictions (strongholds). What is your default? When life triggers a response, what or who do you turn to?

Some men just assume that they have huge sexual appetites that require large amounts of sexual release, when in reality their body is simply looking for a way out or an escape. Many men will use anything sexual to escape for a minute to get their minds off of life, stress, work, and bills so they can detox emotionally. You can be running a thousand miles per hour, but as soon as you get by yourself and slow down here comes temptation.

We cannot allow our fleshly desires to dominate our lives. Regardless of how deep you may feel that you are in this vicious cycle, the blood of Jesus and the Word of God will prevail.

Chapter 2

The Identification Zone

This chapter is very important, and I strongly recommend that you read through it thoroughly and carefully. We are going to take a journey together to uncover in your life where the enemy first ensnared your mind. We must first identify the starting point. If we don't get down to the core issue of how this mindset was adopted, you'll never truly get free. Men don't wake up addicted to sex, pornography, or masturbation; it happens over a process of time. A person has simply fed their flesh too long, and a stronghold has been established. This will take some courage on your part to be honest and transparent. I am here for you and looking forward to your triumphant outcome through Christ.

Fill in the blanks below. Check all that may apply:

1. Does your biological father have a history of sexual perversion? ☐ Yes ☐ No

2. Have you ever had sex? □ Vaginal □ Oral □ Anal

3. How old were you when you had your first sexual encounter?_____

4. Which of the following do you struggle with? □ Pornography □ Masturbation □ Sex □ Other (please specify) _____

5. At what age did you begin to struggle with the above answer? _____

6. How has this sexual issue plagued your life? _

   _____

   _____

   _____

   _____

7. What does freedom mean to you? _____

   _____

   _____

   _____

   _____

8. Have you ever been: □ molested □ raped □ sexual abuse of any kind

   a. If yes, what age? _____

   b. What was your relationship to the person that sexually abused you? _____

   c. Have you forgiven them? □ Yes □ No

d. Do you believe that you should forgive them? □ Yes □ No

e. Why or Why not? _____

_____

_____

_____

(**Note**: Forgiveness does not exonerate the person from the injustice that they have committed. It isn't only morally unacceptable; it is also punishable by law.)

9. Do you feel an attraction to the same sex? □ Yes □ No

a. If yes, do you wish that these thoughts and feelings would go away? □ Yes □ No

b. Why or why not? _____

_____

_____

_____

10. Why do you want to be free? _____

_____

_____

_____

Chapter 3

Generational Curses

"...visiting the iniquity of the fathers upon the children, and upon the children's children, unto the third and to the fourth generation." Exodus 34:7

We naturally pick up the habits and traits of our parents or family members, whether we realize it or not. Mannerisms and styles of speech can often be traced back to your childhood environment. Sin operates the same way; it is easier for you to fall into the same traps as your parents because of conditioning. Whether your parents realized it or not, you observed how they coped with pain, handled circumstances, and dealt with temptations, which created a model of behavior for you. The way you naturally view life is through the experiences and circumstances of your childhood, unless you renew your mind through the Word. It's very rare that you will see a wealthy child move out of their parent's mansion and go find an apartment in Section 8. Why? It was because their upbringing introduced them to a better living environment. The next time you are around your family members, listen to them, ask them about their life and see if you don't find some of those same traits manifesting in you.

In the same manner that blessings can be passed down from generations, so can curses. The opening scripture in this chapter, Exodus 34:7, reveals the concept of "generational curses." We read here a portion of the guidelines that God gave Israel on how He judged sin. There were several cases in the Old Testament where not only was a man judged but his entire household. Thank God we are no longer controlled by the law but rather by grace. However, there are spiritual laws that have been established that grace cannot erase. The grace of God does restore, but it doesn't always keep judgment from coming. I have good news for you! Through the blood of Jesus you can reverse the curse and prohibit it from continuing any longer in your lineage.

Now, let's talk about how to reverse the curse! I want you to look closely at Exodus 34:7. Let's bring some clarity and understanding on how this works. The verse said "visiting the iniquity." When we accept Jesus Christ into our hearts to be our Lord and Savior, the Bible tells us in Colossians 1:13-14 that we are delivered from darkness, and Galatians 3:13 says that we are redeemed from the curse. All darkness, all evil, and every sin are stripped from us, and the chains that bind us fall off.

The revelation that Exodus 34:7 reveals is that the sin will come to visit the next generation whether we are saved or not. Remember Matthew 18:18 says, "... Whatsoever ye shall bind on earth shall be bound in heaven: and whatsoever ye shall loose on earth shall be loosed in heaven." This is a spiritual principle. Mankind has the right to allow or stop things in his life; however, when the enemy is allowed in a man's life the enemy is seeking to steal, kill and destroy everything he has including his children (John 10:10). This is why men are so important because they have legal authority over the family in the realm of the spirit.

Do you remember after Mary and Joseph got married, we never read again where supernatural direction was given to Mary. The Lord would deal with Joseph in dreams or angelic visitations because he was the spiritual authority in that household. The same way we can give God permission to run our households is the same way we can give that same access to the devil. I cannot express how important the role of a man is in the family structure. Even men that abandon their children are still held responsible by Almighty God for the success or destruction of their seed.

How do the sins of the father visit the next generation? Again, once the enemy has access he then has permission to visit. Think about it like this, if you give me a key to your house and invite me to come over, I can decide that I want to stop by your house at 2 o'clock in the morning if I want to because I have access. Now you might not be happy about it but you really can't be too upset because you gave me the key.

This is the danger of sin; it wants to invade every area of your life. It's like the guest that wants to walk all through your house being nosey. If you don't learn how to resist the enemy or take a stand against him, you may find yourself fighting the same battle from your family history. You are more aware of this subject than you realize, and I'll prove it to you. When you go for a doctor's visit, some of the first questions the physician will ask you when preparing your health records is, "does your family have a history of xyz?" They understand that you are more prone to genetically inherit symptoms or traits from your family bloodline than from anywhere else. Break the curse and release the blessing.

Chapter 4

Pornography

This chapter is the silent killer that so many men are ashamed to tell anyone about. In my own personal opinion I believe pornography is one of the most powerful addictions ever known to mankind. I say this because most addictions are physical and deal with how a person feels. Pornography not only affects feelings and emotions, but it captivates the mind, the imagination center. It creates a false world in the imagination of the heart and opens the door for satan to darken the soul. As born-again believers, the enemy cannot possess our spirits because the Holy Spirit abides there. The next best thing the enemy seeks to occupy is the soul of man (mind, will and emotions).

When a person watches pornography, they are participating in the act of fornication along with the individuals because the Bible says to look upon another lustfully is equated to already committing adultery in your heart (Matthew 5:28). The individuals that are committing these acts are ungodly, and this is a form of satanic worship. They are bringing glory to the devil through works of darkness.

We as the church should be interceding for their salvation and deliverance, not participating in these works of darkness. By continuing in pornography you will open yourself up for demonic spirits to control your thoughts. DO NOT and I repeat DO NOT allow the enemy to trick you into watching pornography to see if it bothers you or if you can handle this temptation. Every time you watch pornography, you give up your freedom and a stronghold develops. A stronghold is something that has gained control; some would call it an addiction. Once the stronghold has taken root, you will get to the point where you have to watch it and you won't be able to stop. Willpower cannot break a stronghold because it can only be broken by the power of God.

If you read biblical history during the Roman Era, the Romans practiced satanic rituals by having orgies, group sex, and every perverted sexual act as an offering to their gods.[1] I want to uncover another satanic ritual that was performed during these times which is commonly known today as stripping. They would build sanctuaries or temples to these gods, play music and dance naked on the altars.[2] Keep away from all forms, manners, or styles of pornography. As I mentioned in a previous chapter, the devil really has no new tricks. He uses the same tools but just in more modern and appealing ways.

"But I keep under my body, and bring it into
subjection: lest that by any means, when
I have preached to others, I myself should
be a castaway."I Corinthians 9:27

"And even as they did not like to retain God
in their knowledge, God gave them over to
a reprobate mind, to do those things which
are not convenient;" Romans 1:28

After looking up the word "castaway" in the Greek, I noticed that this word is the same word meaning "reprobate" in Romans 1:28.[3] Many ministers have taught that Paul was saying in I Corinthians 9:27 that the word "castaway" referred to being a hypocrite. This isn't accurate, he was actually saying that if he didn't keep his body under he could become a reprobate like the ones he was trying to minister to with the Gospel.

The Internet has become a major prison for a lot of men. It has become the new slave plantation, concentration camp, and torture chamber of our time. Pornography is the greatest enslavement ever known to man, and satan can do it without anyone ever knowing because it takes place in the privacy of someone's home.

I'm sure you have heard of the term "gateway drugs." These are drugs that often lead to more intense and hardcore drugs. Likewise, pornography is a gateway drug because it opens up a space in your imagination that was never supposed to be exposed to evil. After viewing pornography, the lines between reality and fiction become blurred. It creates an appetite for arousal that can never be quenched which makes it addictive.

Your mind is being exposed to a world of lasciviousness. Lasciviousness is lust on steroids. It is a desire that consumes and sets your soul on fire of hell. James 3:6 talks about how your tongue can also be "set on fire of hell." Your mind is a powerful tool, full of creativity and originality like God. When God created man, He made him in His image and after His likeness (Genesis 1:26).

We were given above any other creature created by God the ability to reason and explore within our imagination. This can be a wonderful thing, but in the wrong hands it can be very destructive. We see this in movie plots all of the time where a scientist stumbles upon an extremely lethal explosive, and an evil terrorist threatens to take over the world by using this explosive. Your mind can become a lethal weapon for evil when you allow the terrorist (the devil) to use it to take over your life.

The addiction to pornography sets in when your imagination begins to explore more creative ways of pleasure. Your mind becomes a laboratory where an evil spirit begins testing and sampling ideas in your imagination and you start wondering, "What does that look like, how does that feel, how can I reach a longer orgasm, etc.?" The devil does not create anything new but rather perverts everything from its original intent.

Just like the Holy Spirit in scripture is referred to as the "all-consuming fire" which burns away the chaff and everything that is not like God, so the enemy has a consuming fire called lasciviousness that ignites wickedness and every vile imagination. Demon spirits begin to linger in your home polluting and intoxicating the very environment with evil imaginations.

In your mind the enemy will come up with every rational reason for watching pornography... "You have sexual needs. Well at least you aren't having sex. You aren't hurting anybody. Nobody at church will ever know. You can't get anyone pregnant." If you don't deal with those thoughts, satan will wage war in your mind to get you to yield to temptation so that the doors of entrapment are now open.

For example, if you're watching something X-rated and now your private part is standing at attention, what do you do? Your body is on fire at this point. You don't have time to pray, read or call a friend. Now here comes the devil to take you even further into a trap of masturbation or sex. For most of you reading this book, this is the vicious cycle of your life.

Here's the reality of this situation, you can't build up all this steam and never release the pressure. Your mind is creating an appetite for your flesh, and you are eventually going to act out in some sexual way. Sometimes those sexual fires of hell will give birth to heinous acts such as incest, molestation, rape, or sodomy. You don't ever want the enemy to use you to destroy someone's life because you wouldn't resist him. The devil cannot fully operate in this earth realm like he wants to without human assistance. He needs someone to cooperate with his agenda. He needs a mind, hands, feet, eyes and ears to carry out his destruction. He requires a human body. Don't yield to the devil. James 4:7 says, "Submit yourselves therefore to God. Resist the devil, and he will flee from you."

Chapter 5

Masturbation

If ever there was a divided topic amongst Christian men, it most definitely is the topic of whether masturbation is a sin. I have been saved a long time and have heard just about every argument imaginable about the subject. Some have said that the act isn't sinful as long as your thoughts aren't sinful during the act of masturbation. I have done some research on the subject and will prove that both the act of masturbation and the thoughts during the act are sinful.

We must first identify where this word 'masturbate' came from. You will never find this word in the Bible because the origin of this word was formulated some time during the 1800's. So, does the Bible reference anything remotely close to the act of masturbation? The Bible does mention the open door to masturbation in Genesis 38:9-10 with the story of a man named Onan. Onan had a brother who died and left a wife with no children. It was customary in those days for the widow of a brother, with no children, to marry the other living brother so that the name of the family would continue. Let's read what happened to Onan out of two different translations to get the fullness of the story.

"But Onan was not willing to have a child who would not be his own heir. So whenever he had intercourse with his brother's wife, he spilled the semen on the ground. This prevented her from having a child who would belong to his brother. But the Lord considered it evil for Onan to deny a child to his dead brother. So the Lord took Onan's life, too." Genesis 38:9-10 (New Living Translation)

"And Onan knew that the seed should not be his; and it came to pass, when he went in unto his brother's wife, that he spilled it on the ground, lest that he should give seed to his brother. And the thing which he did displeased the Lord: wherefore he slew him also." Genesis 38:9-10 (KJV)

It is very important that we understand specifically what displeased the Lord. It was not that Onan took his deceased brother's wife; it was the fact that he withdrew his penis from her vagina and ejaculated on the ground. This is so important! From that moment even to this day, in the medical field the term for what took place in this passage is called "onanism." Onanism is defined as "withdrawal of the penis in sexual intercourse so that ejaculation takes place outside the vagina."[1] You will find listed beside any dictionary definition of this word the synonym masturbation.

Over time men began to find other creative ways to ejaculate without stimulation of the vagina. Onanism is the umbrella for which other sexual acts originated outside of the body. The word "masturbation" was derived from the Latin word "masturbari" which means "the stimulation or manipulation of one's own genitals, especially to orgasm."[2] Masturbation then began to take on forms of its own such as frottage meaning "the practice of getting sexual stimulation and satisfaction by rubbing against something, especially another person"[3] and auto-fellatio which is "the act of oral stimulation of one's own penis as a form of masturbation."[4]

The most interesting part of how the word "masturbation" came about was its root origin [from

Latin masturbārī, of unknown origin; formerly thought to be derived from *manus* hand + *stuprāre* to defile]. The word has been understood in Latin to mean "to defile by the hands." Another interesting thing was the second half of the Latin word *stuprāre* which is from the word *stuprum* meaning "defilement and dishonor" but also related to the word *stupere* meaning "to be stunned or stupefied; to make stupid."[5]

> "If any man defile the temple of God, him shall
> God destroy; for the temple of God is holy,
> which temple ye are." I Corinthians 3:17

Here's the bottom line... God's original intent was that man was supposed to be pleased sexually by his wife only. Even though our society has come up with new and creative ways to reach an orgasm as men, whether you're married or single, you are never supposed to stimulate your own penis. Even if you are married, I Corinthians 7:4 says, "...and likewise also the husband hath not power of his own body, but the wife."

For married men, even if your wife is pregnant and has reached full-term and sexual options become limited or you're away from your wife on a trip, it is still NOT okay for you to masturbate in any way. I Corinthians 7:4

clearly identifies that your body belongs to the wife, not another woman, not your hands, not Vaseline or other lubricants. YOUR WIFE!

Now if you and your wife find creative ways to please one another, Hebrews 13:4 says, "Marriage is honourable in all, and the bed undefiled…" But notice it said "marriage," you can't be married by yourself or else you would be considered single. Therefore you can't have sex by yourself. The other point to the word "marriage" is that you must be married to the person that's stimulating your penis. If you allow anyone other than the woman you are married to, to stimulate you in any way, the other half of Hebrews 13:4 has a warning for you, "…but whoremongers and adulterers God will judge."

For us single brothers, there is absolutely nothing that should be going on sexually in our lives. Period. We must get back to what the Word of God has to say, not society. I am going to help us all in the next couple of chapters, especially single men, about catching things at the thought level. Single brothers, these chapters are vital to your complete freedom. Married men can let off their sexual steam in the bedroom with their wife, but we have to keep our little kettles off the stove completely.

"Can a man take fire in his bosom, and his clothes not be burned?" Proverbs 6:27

I didn't write this book to patty cake and dance around the realities of life. For men, whether you are married or single, it's one thing to battle thoughts but you're in a whole different arena when you start allowing your private parts to start jumping in the fight. So now you've got lustful thoughts and sexual arousal challenging the Word that you have hidden in your heart. If you don't have the Word of God to combat this, I guarantee you will lose every single time. Psalm 119:11 says, "Thy word have I hid in mine heart, that I might **NOT** sin against thee."

Nocturnal Emissions (Wet Dreams)

I have heard many men say that wet dreams are a normal experience outside of the initial puberty stage if you are not having sex. I beg to differ. The initial release of sperm is the sign that puberty has taken place in a young man. From this moment forward a man has erections and the ability to ejaculate. The reason why I personally believe that wet dreams are not pure and must be worked on through renewal of the mind is because of the contents of those dreams. The content by which this bodily function occurs comes through perverse dreams. I would completely agree with the theory held by many that this is just a normal bodily function if there was no association of lust. To say that lust is normal is to say that we don't have control over our subconscious, and satan can just fill us with perverted thinking. To give normalcy to being a victim of lust is to deny the power of the Word of God. When a man wakes up from a sexual dream usually there is a strong desire to have sex.

While a person is asleep, their subconscious is bringing up secret desires and true passions that they may not have acted upon while they're awake. Nocturnal emissions are more than a bodily function because it's exposing what has been planted in the heart. There are also times when the devil will try to interrupt your sleep with perverted dreams. You must begin to immediately take authority over these dreams once you wake up or become aware that they are happening. Take note of Matthew 12:43-45, which explains how when a spirit has departed that it comes back to the house where it once occupied. The enemy will try to creep in through your subconscious. As you begin to resist the enemy with the Word of God as I will teach later on in the book, you will be able to close your dreams off from the devil.

Sexual Dreams

All sexual dreams that come to your mind are not always your fault. There are times when you may have closed the door to perversion in your life, and the enemy may try to see if you would grant him access. There could also be someone that is having impure motives towards you and may even be lusting over you which can be a form of witchcraft. Believe it or not some people may be masturbating, touching themselves sexually, or even having sex with someone else but thinking about you. You do have authority over your dreams. Make this confession according to Proverbs 3:24, "When thou liest down, thou shalt not be afraid: yea, thou shalt lie down, and thy sleep shall be sweet."

> I resist all perverse and wicked dreams sent by the enemy to disturb my sleep. The Holy Spirit is the captain of my dreams, and He alone shows me things to come. satan, you will not have any part of my mind or subconscious. I plead the blood of Jesus over my dreams in Jesus Name, Amen.

Chapter 6

Fornication: Is It Really Love?

Love is one of the most misunderstood and misinterpreted words in the human language. We all have a desire to be loved, but the love we seek is from another human that is incapable of perfection. We place expectations on individuals to give us only what the Father is capable of providing. Now here is where the deception can enter in your life, you say that you are looking for someone to love you, but instead you end up compromising the love you were looking for to fulfill a sexual desire. We say we wanted love but ended up having sex. In the end did you really get the love you were seeking?

Love doesn't mean sex, and sex doesn't mean love. It's really pretty simple if you just look at the definition of both words. Neither one of these words are synonyms. If you say you genuinely love someone you will not put them in a spiritually detrimental position by having sex just because your flesh has not been crucified with Christ.

The only way to avoid fornication is to build boundaries in your life. You must set standards of holiness in your interaction with women or you will fall prey. There are a lot of men that come into the kingdom of God and really don't know where to start on this journey and how to properly interact with the opposite sex in a holy and godly manner. I have listed a few things that are not necessarily sinful if you do them, but they can open the door to sex quickly.

These are some basic guidelines and boundaries to avoid fornication. This is not a section on dating so I would advise you to get other material if you want to know how to date in a godly manner.

1. There should be no reason under any circumstance that you should have a woman over your place or you go over to her place alone to talk. There are so many public places that you can go to that are private and don't cost any money. You want to avoid the appearance of evil. To have a young lady walking from

your place of residence alone could give the impression that intimacy has taken place.

2. You have no reason to ever need to see a young ladies bedroom, or vice versa where she needs to see yours. Do not even put yourself in that position because it is like leading a sheep to the slaughter. If you follow the first boundary you don't ever have to even worry about 'what if's' because you wouldn't be there at all.

3. Avoid going out of town with a young lady if there is no one else there to hold you accountable. You should never stay in the same hotel room. Even be careful on long road trips together; bring someone along. These are very common pitfalls that can lead to fornication.

4. Monitor how often you kiss a woman on the lips or even if you should kiss at all in the relationship. You know how you are and what you can handle and most men can't handle just having a simple kiss at the end of the date and going home. If a kiss on the lips is sending you into frenzy then you just need to give her a nice kiss on the cheek and go home.

5. Never tongue kiss because this is a form of foreplay that will cause arousal and stimulation. This should only be experienced in the marriage covenant.

6. Affection is not a bad thing; however, keep physical contact to a minimal. Putting your arms around her shoulder or waist is fine, holding hands is cool but really let that be the extent to which you both are having physical contact. If involved in dancing or other activities that require contact, make sure there is a little space between you two. For us as men, we can become so easily aroused by the touch of a woman. Don't allow this physical contact to turn into a form of foreplay. You might think you are good and can handle yourself but when a woman that you are attracted to touches your body, arousal can happen almost immediately.

7. As a believer, your motivation in getting to know a young lady is to interview her as a potential mate. Even if you both decide to dissolve the relationship, she should be left whole and not emotionally damaged because you crossed so many lines.

8. Unless you are in pre-marital counseling or you have proposed to her, casual conversations about sex should be off limits. We are very visual beings and conversations about sex can open up the imagination and light a sexual fire within us.

Chapter 7

Adultery

This chapter is specifically for married men who have either cheated on their spouse or may be leaning in that direction. You need to first identify what's going on in the marriage that is causing a disconnection in the relationship. Adultery will ultimately destroy your entire life, and I do mean every aspect of your life. This is a breaking of covenant that comes with impending judgment. You should never for one split second even consider this, especially if you have children. Children are the ones who suffer the most, and they can experience lifelong damaging effects because of it. If you were not delivered from a promiscuous lifestyle, marriage is and can never be a cure for lust. Lust cannot be cured; it must be obliterated through the power of the Word of God.

Oftentimes affairs don't start off physical in nature because you first connect emotionally. The reason why affairs are so dangerous is because it's almost as if you have allowed yourself to enter the dating scene all over again with someone else. Do you remember the excitement you felt when you first met your wife? You are stepping back into that space of excitement and curiosity with someone else.

An emotional affair is always more destructive to a marriage than just a physical fling. One of the biggest lies that the devil will tell any married man is that they can get away with it without anyone finding out. LIE. LIE. LIE. The Bible says that your sins will find you out. God will not be unrighteous to that wife while you're being unfaithful. The deceiving part about adultery is that you don't always get caught right away, so you play around with the grace of God. You make excuses for what you're doing, and it seems fun for a season.

Marriage is work and requires commitment and dedication. You must fight for your marriage. There are so many obstacles that a marriage must overcome in just bringing together two completely different people with opposite ways of doing things. Don't allow the enemy to destroy your household because you won't deal with lust. I promise you it will come for your marriage in some form or another.

Lust can never be quenched. It is like a cancer that eats away at everything good in your life. At the end of the day it all comes down to how bad you want to live right before the Lord and be a great example for your family. You don't entertain women that want to flirt with you. Keep yourself in the love of God and in the Word. Make sure you get to the last chapters in this book and begin to use your spiritual weapons to defeat this thing.

You may also need to go in for counseling to see where there may be a breakdown in your relationship with your wife. Examine what's deficient in your relationship. What do you need from your wife that you feel you're not getting? Sit down and discuss with your wife what you need from her. She's not a mind reader, and we as men definitely can't tell what's going on with women. It takes open, honest and non-judgmental communication. What you want her to do for you must be reciprocated into what she needs. Her needs aren't going to be the same thing as what you need.

You can sum men up into four basic needs: money, sex, food, and peace. If we have an abundance of these four things, we are generally pretty happy campers. For women, their list may be ten or twenty things. If you think that marriage consists of having sex all day, you are sadly mistaken my brother.

First Signs

You need to take the initial thought of adultery captive. I have heard people say, "It's okay to window shop as long as you don't buy anything." This way of thinking is detrimental because "window shopping" creates a desire for something that your flesh will eventually find a way to purchase. Ephesians 4:27 reminds us to, "Neither give place to the devil." By entertaining thoughts of intimacy or even wondering what it would be like to be with someone else, you are giving a space for the enemy to divide and destroy the unity in your marriage.

One of the easiest ways to divide a marriage is through dissatisfaction. The older people would say it like this, "the grass always looks greener on the other side until you get over there and find out that it's Astroturf." The enemy will bring up every flaw or idiosyncrasy that is in your mate to cause dissatisfaction. If you don't check that spirit, you will stop noticing the benefit and blessing that she is to your life. This fantasy woman that you have conjured in your mind does not exist.

The other woman that you're noticing has issues too, maybe even worse than your wife. As my grandmother would say, "don't jump out the frying pan and into the fire." You think you're escaping one thing only to find yourself in a more tragic situation.

You might have gotten bored in your marriage. Well you know what; it's time to spice it up. Do something spontaneous with your wife. If you have smaller children, make sure you are still taking time to be away with your wife only. Marriage is work, but most importantly it's a decision of love. You have to decide what you want in your marriage and speak the Word of God. We can easily quote a scripture for healing or finances, but think about how often you confess the Word over your wife and the health of your marriage. The Word of God will keep the enemy at bay. Whatever you don't like about your marriage, it is your responsibility to change it as the head of the household. Decree what you want to see in your marriage.

We as men have a governing authority over our households. If the devil is wreaking havoc in your home, it's your fault. If there was a known robber in your neighborhood, would you leave your front door wide open at night? I know that sounds crazy, doesn't it? Don't laugh too soon because most of us do the same thing in our spiritual life.

John 10:10 says, "The thief cometh not, but for to steal, and to kill, and to destroy..." satan is the known robber in the world, so why would we give him access to our lives by leaving our minds wide open? Anytime you entertain thoughts of adultery, you're opening the door for the thief to come steal from you, and he doesn't just want to tear up your marriage. He wants your finances, your peace of mind and your children. Keep the enemy out by speaking forth the Word, and spend more time praying in the Spirit.

Chapter 8

Homosexuality

This has to be one of the most sensitive subjects for any man to deal with but yet it is so real and requires love, compassion, and patience in helping men to overcome. Many have failed in trying to minister to men dealing with same-sex attractions because of fear tactics, mind manipulation, shame, embarrassment, etc. Love has to be the motivating factor in everything that we do and this issue is no different. If you are struggling with same-sex attractions, the first thing you must never forget is that the Father loves you and has open arms to receive you. Never let anyone tell you differently. The enemy would want you to stray away from God because of condemnation, but God is truly the only one that can deliver and set free.

"But if a man, without being forced to do so, has firmly made up his mind not to marry, and if he has his will under complete control and has already decided in his own mind what to do—then he does well not to marry..." I Corinthians 7:37 (Good News Translation)

You may say Onesimus, "I just don't have an attraction towards women in a physical way." Let me be the first to tell you that's okay. We just read here in the aforementioned scripture that if you can keep the desire for sex under control, you're fine if you never marry. Some have even taught that if you don't feel attracted to women that something is wrong and you are evil. The issue with homosexuality is the same as with fornication, it is the sin of lusting and sexual activity. The driving force behind homosexuality is the desire to have sex with another man.

When those thoughts come, what are you doing with them? Before you ever have sex with someone, you premeditate the act. If you are letting them continue to linger in your mind, they will eventually become an unquenchable fire within your flesh.

"And likewise also the men, leaving the natural use of the woman, burned in their lust one toward another; men with men working that which is unseemly, and receiving in themselves that recompence of their error which was meet. And even as they did not like to retain God in their knowledge, God gave them over to a reprobate mind, to do those things which are not convenient;" Romans 1:27-28

I don't want to spend a whole lot of time talking about how homosexuality is a sin. It is clearly evident in the Word, and most Christians have heard this from day one of salvation. I want to focus on how to get free. This chapter is not for individuals that want to debate and rationalize and make excuses for sin. I am here to help those who truly want to be delivered.

Sexual urges towards other men does not give a person the right to have sex; this is the exact same sin as fornication. Sex was created between husband (man) and wife (woman). Take my life for example, I am a virgin. Just because I have a desire to be with a woman does not give me the right to violate the Word of God and become promiscuous. The same thing with you, no matter what thoughts or feelings you may have, you can't just have sex with a man because you feel gay. The same scriptures that I have applied over my life to keep my flesh crucified will work for you as well. When a lustful thought comes to your mind about another man, you must cast it down. I explain this process in Chapters 14 and 17.

I'm going to tell you something that may be of a shock to you. Don't spend a whole lot of time trying to figure out how to fix yourself. Allow the Word of God to cleanse your mind. You absolutely want to come out of any relationship or environment that is promoting sin; however, your main focus needs to be on Jesus. Spend time in prayer, reading the Word, praying in the Spirit, and worshipping God. Get as close to God as your next breath. He said "Come unto me, all ye that labour and are heavy laden, and I will give you rest" (Matthew 11:28). You don't have to keep begging God to save you from this sin. As you get closer to the presence of God His all-consuming fire begins to burn away every desire, motive and intention that is not like Him.

Learn how to spend time with God just because you love Him. Sin makes us cowards before God because we carry the feeling of disappointment. You may have even told people that's why you're not as strong of a Christian because you feel like a disappointment to God. Christianity is not about getting perfect before you come to Jesus, it' about coming as you are and letting Him perfect you. Don't make excuses for sin or take God for granted.

Here are some ways to stay away from the temptation to have sex. When the temptation comes, these are some basic things you can do to avoid this activity.

1. If you know that another man is dealing with same-sex attractions or actively practicing homosexuality, DO NOT spend time with him by yourself. Whether you feel attracted or not, don't give the enemy any place. If you are attracted, this could lead to fornication, and if you're not attracted this can lead to rape. Don't put yourself in that position.

    •   Until you are completely delivered, you are not strong enough to have associations with other men dealing with homosexuality. You may feel like you can help them and be a witness to them but that sin may end up overtaking you in the process.

    •   You must cut ties with people in this lifestyle. You need time away from anything that would try to reattach itself back to you.

2. If you know of another man or friend that needs help in this area, refer them to a female minister where they can be comfortable and truly get the help they need without distraction.

3. Since you are a man, you can't necessarily escape men but monitor your intention of being with men. Make sure your interactions are with a pure motive.

4. Avoid seeing men naked, whether you're attracted or not. You don't want to give the enemy any ammunition against you. As a man, you have access to see other men in more of a private setting such as a locker room, gym, pool area, etc. If you cannot handle these environments, wait until other men have left before entering.

Chapter 9

Evil in the Shadows

This chapter is not intended to scare anyone but to inform you of the value of your decisions and how they can affect you spiritually. Every decision that we make in the natural has a spiritual consequence, whether it leads to good or evil.

"Be not deceived; God is not mocked: for whatsoever a man soweth, that shall he also reap." Galatians 6:7

"For he who sows to his own flesh (lower nature, sensuality) will from the flesh reap decay and ruin and destruction, but he who sows to the Spirit will from the Spirit reap eternal life." Galatians 6:8 (Amplified Bible)

Notice in Galatians 6:8 in the Amplified Bible that the end result of following the flesh will result in decay, ruin, and destruction. Now I don't know which one of those three words sounds the worst, but it seems as though nothing good comes out of the flesh (Romans 7:18). Following the flesh will cause you to sin, and sin is the open invitation for satan to come in and set up shop in your life. As a born-again believer, satan has no legal access to you because now you have been delivered from his kingdom and made new in Christ (Colossians 1:13-14; II Corinthians 5:17).

The entry point for satan is when we stop walking according to the spirit and begin to indulge in the flesh (Galatians 5:16). The enemy begins to work in that sin like a boa constrictor. When a boa constrictor first grabs a hold of something, the animal or person can still breathe and function. However, the key to the success of this snake is not its bite but its ability to squeeze and constrict its prey to the point of suffocation.

This is where the enemy is very cunning and deceptive in his approach. You may have started off playing around with certain sexual things such as masturbation, pornography, or light sex, and you are convinced in your mind that you can stop anytime you get ready. How many times have you told yourself, "I promise, I'm only going to do this one more time?" And then that one more time turns into one more time.

Instead of getting into the Word of God and renewing your mind, you allow this boa constrictor to continue to squeeze and constrict to the point of suffocation. What you don't realize is that one day you will wake up and find out that you can't breathe. This addiction has now smothered you, and you are walking around with a boa constrictor completely wrapped around your soul. If you continue to sin you keep feeding this evil spirit, and it gets bigger, stronger and heavier.

This is no longer just a lust of the flesh because a spirit of lust has now taken residence in your soul. You cannot be completely possessed by the devil because your spirit belongs to God; however, your soul (mind, will and emotions) can be overcome by satanic powers. Now this spirit is telling **you** what to do.

It tells you to watch pornography, masturbate, or fornicate. It torments you in your dreams. Your dreams are very sexually explicit and perverse. You have lost control of your mind and your natural sexual limitations. Now you need to see more, do more, have more, and feel more. What you have been doing is no longer enough to get you excited anymore. Anything that is sexual excites you. It's almost as if you have turned into an addict waiting for your next sexual fix.

You can't look at people in their eye because this spirit begins to undress them in your mind. This is what the scriptures refer to as a stronghold. In later chapters I will give you practical steps and things to help you get free and stay free because there is enough power in the blood of Jesus to eradicate every work of the enemy.

"When the unclean spirit is gone out of a man, he walketh through dry places, seeking rest, and findeth none. Then he saith, I will return into my house from whence I came out; and when he is come, he findeth it empty, swept, and garnished. Then goeth he, and taketh with himself seven other spirits more wicked than himself, and they enter in and dwell there: and the last state of that man is worse than the first. Even so shall it be also unto this wicked generation." Matthew 12:43-45

As the Scripture identified, evil spirits need a home. They are spirit beings that can't express themselves in this natural realm because they don't have a body. The enemy is looking for a home. Make up in your mind that satan will not have anything in you. Once he finds something in you that belongs to him, then he will hook you in and drag you wherever he wants to take you. Sin belongs to the enemy, and he has every right to come after it if it's in your life.

Sexual Perversion

The online dictionary defines perversion or to pervert as: "to lead astray morally, to turn away from the right course, to lead into mental error or false judgment; to turn to an improper use; misapply."[1] When a person engages in sexual perversion, they are engaging in activity that is anti-God or against God's way. It is a misapplied or misdirected use of sexual pleasure.

Sin will always take you further than you want to go, keep you longer than you want to stay, and make you pay more than you are willing to pay.

"You have proved my heart; You have visited me in the night; You have tried me and find nothing [no evil purpose in me]..." Psalm 17:3 (Amplified Bible)

We have been so desensitized by the media that we are sexual beings who need to express ourselves and whatever feels good, do it. Unfortunately this has led us so far astray and into very dangerous territory. God is not just telling us to abstain from evil just because He doesn't want us to enjoy life. God understands that when we engage in sin, we come from under His protection and become defenseless in our fight with the enemy. The thief then has a right to come in to steal, kill, and destroy (John 10:10).

Adjust

Chapter 10

Release the Pain and Forgive

Usually addictions are a way to escape from something or someone. We as men can become involved in very destructive behaviors when we are hurting on the inside. There are times where you must ask yourself, "What am I running from? Who am I running from? What am I turning to?" You didn't arrive at this place by yourself; the enemy has used some situation in your life to either physically, mentally, or emotionally damage or drive you into this harmful behavior. It's time to take the shackles of hurt and pain off and reclaim your freedom in Christ.

Forgiveness is one of the essential keys to your freedom. First, you must identify if there is anyone in your life who you have not forgiven. You may say, "Onesimus I just can't forgive them. You don't know what they've done to me or how badly they've wounded me." I am in no way downplaying the damage that has come to you, but by not letting it go you forever stay locked away in their prison. The power to break free is in being able to forgive. All the nights that you have cried, felt worthless and been angry over what has happened to you has not resolved the inner wounds of your heart. You think you're free but you're really not. The thoughts and the memories are all tools that the enemy uses against you to kill your confidence.

"For whatsoever is born of God overcometh the world: and this is the victory that overcometh the world, even our faith." I John 5:4

"...faith which worketh by love." Galatians 5:6

We can overcome any and every thing through faith in the Word. Faith comes through welcoming the Word of God into the heart but that does not mean that it will work automatically. Your faith can be present but be in a dormant state because love is absent. It's like turning your car on but the gear is in park. You can press the gas pedal all day long and rev your engine, but there can be no movement until the gear is put in drive. The love of God is what gives your faith access to unlock the power that rests on His Word.

When we operate in unforgiveness, the key of faith will not work, and we remain locked out of the door God has for us. Many of us remain locked out of God's best because we've allowed our emotions to overrule our spirit. It's just like an employee that comes to work every day, but when they get there they sit at their desk all day long and do nothing, yet the employer keeps paying them to come to work. What good is faith if it's showing up, but you can't get it to do anything for you?

I Forgive Me

Forgiveness is not just in reference to another person. There are times where you need to forgive yourself. You might have failed so many times that it's hard for you to forgive yourself. Anytime you yield to the voice of condemnation, it will attack your righteous position and challenge your forgiveness of yourself. God's grace and mercy caused you to see another day because He wants you to know that you deserve another chance.

What does it mean to forgive youself? After you confess your sins to God according to I John 1:9 and truly repent and turn from it, you now have to deal with the condemnation. It's when you deal with condemnation that you have truly forgiven yourself. By forgiving yourself you are saying that if God has forgiven me and cast my sins from me then I accept His forgiveness, and I stand clean and washed in the blood of Jesus.

Condemnation has a very subtle way of eating at the very core of who you are and destroys the image of who God has called you to be. It attacks your strength of being a man. As men we have this conquering nature about us; we don't like to lose. The devil knows this so he works on that condemnation with thoughts like: I thought you were a Christian, how could you have done something like this?; What would happen if people from your church ever found out what you've been struggling with?; How in the world are you going to witness to somebody about Jesus when you aren't even living it?; God can't use you now, look how messed up you are. Condemnation kills confidence!

Walking in Love

When you step outside of love, you step outside of the safety and protection of God. God is love. He does not just have a characteristic of love, He is love personified. We forfeit the ability of God to work in our life when we operate in offense. James 3:16 says "For where envying and strife is, there is confusion and every evil work." The enemy wants us to hold on to bitterness and strife so he can have access. Offense gets you on the devil's turf, and he doesn't play fair. The enemy is after the same place where you love God from which is your heart. He wants to take God's place and fill you with hatred and strife. What makes poison so deadly are the toxins that it contains. The longer poison sits, the more destructive it becomes. By holding on to pain, the more destructive it becomes to you.

> "For as he thinketh in his heart,
> so is he..." Proverbs 23:7

The heart is the place where you believe from because it houses your core thoughts. If the enemy can get you to believe negatively about yourself or someone else, then that's how you will respond. Your spirit is equipped to produce or make manifest what you believe.

Do you see now why the enemy fights to keep you holding on to the past and deadly emotions? The enemy doesn't have the same access into our lives like sinners. Unbelievers are under the rule of satan. The only way the devil can destroy a believer is by getting the believer to sabotage themselves. You may think you are getting back at whoever has done you wrong, but you are only delaying your own progress and opening the door for satan. It is like taking a fully loaded weapon and pulling the trigger on yourself. You really can't afford to be in strife because it causes your prayers to be hindered. Did you know that your answer to prayer is based on your willingness to walk in forgiveness?

"And when ye stand praying, forgive, if ye have ought against any: that your Father also which is in heaven may forgive you your trespasses. But if ye do not forgive, neither will your Father which is in heaven forgive your trespasses." Mark 11:25-26

Love is Not Trust

Read I Corinthians 13:4-8, it didn't say love was trusting. Trust has to be developed through actions and experience. If a person's behavioral pattern is consistently detrimental then love says I'm not going to hold anything against you, but I can't trust that your character is developed enough for interaction with me. You have to see yourself as a precious commodity. You wouldn't just leave diamonds in the ash tray of your car, so don't allow people to put you somewhere you don't belong. You don't belong in abuse, neglect, fear, bondage, hurt, or strife. You have to make up in your mind that, "I love you, but you aren't about to put me in the ash tray."

> "And be ye kind one to another, tenderhearted,
> forgiving one another, even as God for Christ's
> sake hath forgiven you." Ephesians 4:32

How do I know if I am genuinely walking in love with my neighbor? You know by examining your heart. What comes to your mind when you think of this person? Is it kind and forgiving? If not, pray the prayer of forgiveness at the end of this chapter and make the Love Confession in the back of this book so the Word can uproot any strife in your heart. You don't want the devil to have place in you.

Now don't put yourself in that position again with that person. Individuals do have the ability to change, and you should give them the space to change. Don't just go off of their potential, you need to see the manifested fruit of change. Without the fruit of change that person is more than likely going to hurt you again because hurting people hurt other people.

If there is a case of abuse of any kind, the best thing is to stay away from that person completely unless there is a major heart transformation. No one deserves to be abused physically, sexually, mentally, or emotionally. If you are suffering abuse in your home, please contact someone and reach out for help. If you are dealing with abuse in your marriage, seek counseling immediately because all men have a breaking point and you may one day explode and not even realize what you're doing. It's time for you to live in peace because you deserve it!

Prayer of Forgiveness for Others:

Father in the Name of Jesus, I come before your throne of grace asking for Your help and assistance in my time of need. I have been done wrong by _____, and their actions have hurt me. I recognize that we don't fight against flesh and blood; they were just being used by the enemy to inflict pain in my life. I forgive them and release them as You have commanded me in your Word. Father God, be the balm of Gilead and allow your healing to become an ointment over every wound that has come as a result. Restore my soul right now God. Heal every emotion. Set me free. In Jesus' Name, Amen.

Prayer of Forgiveness for Yourself:

Father in the Name of Jesus, I come before Your throne of grace asking for Your forgiveness and mercy. I repent for allowing condemnation to replace my faith in what Your Word has said about me. Forgive me for walking around depressed over the sins of my past that You have already forgiven and forgotten. This day I accept Your forgiveness and open my heart to receive Your compassion towards me. You love me, and I love you back with all of my heart in Jesus Name, Amen.

Chapter 11

Repentance and the Grace to Overcome Sin

There have been various teachings in recent years on the grace of God. Some have assessed that the word "grace" is universal in the scriptures and has the same meaning in every place. In the New Testament, we see Paul use this term quite frequently in many different scenarios and relating to various things. However, in this reading I want to discuss the "grace" that is available to us as believers to overcome sin.

In the Old Testament under the law, there was no grace for sin. Jesus had not died nor was His blood shed for the remission of sin. In those times, if someone sinned they were immediately judged with the harshest of consequences. The law was very rigid and did not give allowances for sin. Once Jesus came and took our place on the Cross, He did not cancel out the law, He came to improve it. Jesus made it possible for us to successfully live in obedience to the law. After He arose from the grave and presented His blood before God on the mercy seat (Hebrews 10:10-12), this is what gave us access "to come boldly to the throne of grace, that we may obtain mercy, and find grace to help in time of need" according to Hebrews 4:16. This grace has been provided to be a buffer between us and immediate judgment and keeps us from receiving the full consequences for our actions.

> "Moreover the law entered, that the offence might abound. But where sin abounded, grace did much more abound:" Romans 5:20

Thank God that His grace is there when we need it for our lives. Where would we be without this grace? We serve a loving and merciful Father who is full of compassion and slow to anger.

The Parameters of Grace

Grace has been granted by Jesus' blood, not our own works. However, this grace comes with regulations and parameters. Even though we know that grace does abound, we can never use this grace as a license to keep sinning. In some aspects we already subconsciously take the grace of God for granted because we haven't seen judgment show up in certain areas of our life. This tends to deceive us in not dealing with certain problem areas in our life as quickly as we should.

In biblical times, you would've thought long and hard before you just allowed your flesh to run crazy. In those times, depending on what the sin was you could've been exiled from your family, stoned to death, or even beheaded. That's why it tickles me when I hear men say they just can't control themselves. If you knew a thought or action could cost you your life, you would really think twice about whether or not you can control yourself. Even without a scripture, you would find strength in will power alone to keep yourself from committing sin. Remember the story of the woman caught in the act of adultery? The reason why Jesus responded in John 8:7, "...He that is without sin among you, let him first cast a stone at her" is because they were getting ready to kill her according to the law.

What Happens If We Abuse This Grace?

In the New Testament, Paul wrote a letter to the Corinthian church about a man that was fornicating with his father's wife. Paul was disturbed by this because the man had not repented neither did the church address the issue. Paul's response in I Corinthians 5:5 was, "To deliver such a one unto satan for the destruction of the flesh, that the spirit may be saved in the day of the Lord Jesus." What did Paul mean by "deliver such a one unto satan?" This simply means that the grace of God would lift from the man and satan would have access to steal, kill, and destroy (John 10:10).

The aspect of grace that deals with sin is time sensitive. If you notice, the Bible speaks of God's mercy enduring forever, but grace is not forever. In fact right now we are under a dispensation of grace, an allotted time. Soon this age will end, and we will step over into eternity. We can see this clearly in Revelation 2:21, "And I gave her space to repent of her fornication; and she repented not." This is an example of the grace of God being bestowed upon Jezebel. Notice Jesus was speaking here and called it a "space to repent."

You might go further to ask, how long does someone have to get it right? No one ever really knows the answer. God is merciful and full of compassion, and according to your knowledge of the Word of God and your maturity in the things of God, each person's window of grace is different. The main point is this, "...

if we would judge ourselves, we should not be judged" (I Corinthians 11:31).

Let's always remember one important truth which is that sin is not more powerful than the Word of God. The Word of God and the blood of Jesus are the weapons against not only sin but every work of darkness that might try and come upon us. Revelation 12:11 reiterates this truth that we overcome by the blood of Jesus and the Word.

Repentance is not the bad word that most people have made it out to be but it literally means to go in a different direction, to change your mind. It's like driving into a subdivision and one of the streets had a sign that read 'dead end.' To get out you would have to turn around. It's the same way with sin. If you are headed down a dead end path that leads to destruction, you need to go in the opposite direction of that sin. Repentance is the not same as forgiveness, and this is why most people don't get completely free. Asking for forgiveness deals with the sin that has been committed, but repentance is the action that I take to prevent the sin from recurring in the future.

Chapter 12

Conviction vs. Condemnation

One evening while I was washing dishes I heard these words come up in my spirit, "In Romans 8:1 it reads there is therefore now no *condemnation*, it didn't say there is therefore now no *conviction*." I stepped back and immediately grabbed my Bible to read that passage. In that moment I began to realize that many are confusing the conviction in their heart with the condemnation of their mind. Christians have not understood that there is a distinct difference between conviction and condemnation.

As you begin to develop yourself in the Word of God, your spirit will bring a greater level of conviction about areas of your life that need to be adjusted. The Word will sharpen your spirit's ability to distinguish between what is right and wrong. The latter end of Hebrews 4:12 states that the Word, "...is a discerner of the thoughts and intents of the heart." If you disregard the conviction that is in your heart, you will become deceived in your thinking.

You should always check on the inside before you make a decision to see how your spirit may be leading you. Proverbs 20:27 says, "The spirit of man is the candle of the Lord, searching all the inward parts of the belly." Conviction in the life of a believer is a very necessary component towards guidance and direction. This check or warning is there to notify you that the direction you are taking is wrong.

Conviction is the moral compass in your heart. Even before you became born-again your conscience served as a moral compass; however, as you continued to override that innocence you began to lose that sense of right and wrong. Things that you knew were wrong before suddenly didn't seem to bother you. The sin nature began to take over, and your conscious became seared.

Some have said that the Holy Spirit brings conviction, but we don't have evidence in scripture that the Holy Spirit brings conviction to a believer. We read in John 16:8 that the Holy Spirit reproves the world of sin, but He is here to lead, guide and comfort the believer. Conviction comes as an inner prompting or urge from your own spirit.

Now, let's define condemnation. Condemnation is the voice of your feelings which brings guilt, shame, and embarrassment for a shortcoming. It will always attack the character and self-worth of a person. satan's objective in bringing condemnation is to challenge your position of righteousness before God. If Christ has forgiven you and forgotten about it, so should you. Don't tolerate any thoughts that challenge your righteousness and freedom in Christ.

The reason I believe so many Christians struggle with condemnation is because they have not learned how to get free from sin. The biggest issue that I have run across is not so much the condemnation as much as it is the perpetual sin. This is where the enemy is able to gain a stronghold in the mind of believers. Every time you sin, satan takes a hit at your armor of righteousness. The enemy has found a way to keep you trapped in condemnation instead of sonship. In the book of Revelation, satan is referred to as the "accuser of the brethren." Many people are not free because they're trying to work on the condemnation before they uproot the sin in their life. When you eradicate sin, condemnation is easy to address.

"Unto the pure all things are pure: but unto them that are defiled and unbelieving is nothing pure; but even their mind and conscience is defiled." Titus 1:15

You have to be able to identify the difference between conviction and condemnation. If you have missed the mark, repented and made a turn from sin but the thought of it continues to haunt you to a point of not moving forward or feeling inadequate, then this is condemnation. Now if you keep falling in the same area and haven't quite gotten the victory over a particular issue then that is not condemnation rising up but your spirit being grieved about what you're doing. You should never be able to miss the mark and your spirit not check you about the matter. The day you as a believer can sin and nothing in your heart bothers you, your heart has become darkened and you are in a backslidden state. Even though it may not feel good, conviction is a necessary part of having a healthy spiritual life.

"The Lord disciplines everyone he loves. He severely disciplines everyone he accepts as his child." Hebrews 12:6 (God's Word Translation)

"Now no chastening for the present seemeth to be joyous, but grievous: nevertheless afterward it yieldeth the peaceable fruit of righteousness unto them which are exercised thereby." Hebrews 12:11

Chapter 13

Come Out, Separate, and Touch Not

"Wherefore come out from among them, and be ye separate, saith the Lord, and touch not the unclean thing; and I will receive you." II Corinthians 6:17

The Lord identified three very specific things in this passage of scripture that we must take a closer look at: 1) come out from among them, 2) be ye separate, and 3) touch not the unclean thing. This chapter will give some practical steps that must accompany the spiritual aspects of freedom. Freedom is not solely spiritual. There are some natural avenues by which you came into that sin. You must stay away from carnal things or weights that may lead to sin, and we will teach you how in this chapter.

Come out from among Them

> "Be not deceived: evil communications corrupt good manners." I Corinthians 15:33

If the Lord is commanding you to "come out from among them" then that means there are certain people that are causing harm to your walk with Him. You may not notice it at first, but if your friends are influencing you more than you're influencing them, you must walk away from being among them. Let's add some balance to this. Does God mean act arrogant and nasty towards them? Absolutely not, the Lord is simply warning us about not always being in the presence of those that would influence us to live unholy. If they have made a conscious decision that they are going to continue to walk in sin, you just can't be with them on a consistent basis. The sin that your friend may be holding on to will over time weaken your spirit and corrupt your morals.

Be Ye Separate

To sanctify something means to set it apart or section it off from everything else. Some have thought sanctification was about being a super deep Christian and living in the clouds all day. In the simplest of terms, the way you sanctify yourself is to put distance or extract yourself from worldly things. This can be accomplished through fasting; however, Brother Kenneth E. Hagin mentioned something very profound that the Lord shared with him. He said, "If you would live a fasted life you wouldn't need to spend so much time going on fasts." I have come to embrace this revelation for myself, and this approach creates a greater longevity to abstain from carnality.

Have you ever fasted and ended up going back to the very same thing you went on the fast to get away from? Sanctification was never meant to only be a week or month long regimen twice a year. As we continue to grow in God there should be more and more things that we pull away from as we draw closer to Him that we never go back to.

Touch Not the Unclean Thing

"Touch not" is not only talking about physical things, but it means to not touch unclean things in thought, word, and deed. The Lord is instructing us that if we come into contact with anything that is considered unclean or unholy, to not touch it in our thoughts, talk about it with our words, nor act on it in our deeds. Let's break it down a little further.

Thoughts, Words, Deeds

Thoughts – You may see an extremely attractive individual and you immediately notice that they are exactly what you want from head to toe. Noticing an attractive individual is not a sin, but it can become a sin when your thoughts become sexual in nature and you now want to have sexual contact with this person. The thought only becomes unclean when it crosses the boundaries of what is pure (Philippians 4:8). Just because the thought comes does not mean you should meditate on it and allow it to take you to the point of sin.

> "Can a man take fire in his bosom, and his
> clothes not be burned?" Proverbs 6:27

Trust me, I don't care how strong you feel like you may be, if you keep playing with sexual fire you will get burned.

Words – Don't allow anything impure to come out of your mouth for any reason. Sometimes when men get around others guys they tend to talk or joke about inappropriate sexual desires or experiences they have had. Your mouth is a gateway to your spirit. The words that you speak will get into your heart and begin to produce or manifest into a sexual desire that you won't be able to turn off. Your tongue sets the course for your thoughts to follow. We will go into further detail about this in Chapter 14.

"And the tongue is a fire, a world of iniquity: so is the tongue among our members, that it defileth the whole body, and setteth on fire the course of nature; and it is set on fire of hell." James 3:6

"Let no corrupt communication proceed out of your mouth, but that which is good to the use of edifying, that it may minister grace unto the hearers." Ephesians 4:29

Deeds – This refers to anything physical or tangible that you can access through your five senses. Stay away from anything that isn't wholesome or pure. Another word for deeds is actions. Don't even get close to any action that does not reflect the God that lives within you. Here are some examples: sex scenes in movies, porn, naked pictures in a magazine, sex tapes, inappropriate Internet sites, masturbating, hand jobs, sex toys, penis pumps, blow-up dolls, sex of any kind, or anything perverse.

Accountability

> "But now I have written unto you not to keep
> company, if any man that is called a brother
> be a fornicator, or covetous, or an idolator, or
> a railer, or a drunkard, or an extortioner; with
> such an one no not to eat." I Corinthians 5:11

What is Paul saying here? Is he saying that we should not walk in love or be judgmental against our brothers or sisters in Christ? Absolutely not, but he is saying to be mindful of who you associate with in your life. Now that you are born-again, there are some things that you must separate yourself from or sin will drag you back into the person you used to be.

You have left your old friends so who are you supposed to hang out with now? This is the stage where you have to leave your comfort zone and meet new brothers in Christ that are living the born-again life. Some call this finding your 'Accountability Partner.' An accountability partner is a brother in Christ that is motivating you to live the Word and encouraging you to maintain your witness for Christ before the world.

"...to them that have obtained like precious faith with us through the righteousness of God and our Saviour Jesus Christ:" II Peter 1:1

In the above passage, Peter was writing to people that believed as he believed. When searching for other brothers that have "like precious faith," you must consider what they believe about the Word of God and how they conduct their life. If they compromise in their walk with Christ then you must understand that they could never lead you; you must lead them.

Chapter 14

Catch It at the Thought Level

I know I've probably said every chapter in this book is important, but I am about to go into a greater uncovering of what actually takes place within a man during temptation. I will also discuss in this chapter how you DO NOT have to struggle sexually every day. Men have been sold a bunch of lies by the enemy that we are sexual beings who will always struggle in this area. THE DEVIL IS A LIAR! You can live free.

"But I see another law in my members, warring against the law of my mind, and bringing me into captivity to the law of sin which is in my members." Romans 7:23

"However, I see a different standard [at work] throughout my body. It is at war with the standards my mind sets and tries to take me captive to sin's standards which still exist throughout my body." Romans 7:23 (God's Word Translation)

Notice what Paul identified in this passage of scripture, he saw another law within his members or flesh. His body was craving to do what was against his will. We have already discussed renewing our mind and resisting thoughts, but what happens when we don't resist. If we don't deal with the thoughts while they are in our mind then the body will chime in with its own agenda. We are created a triune being: spirit, soul, body. You are a spirit, you have a soul and you live in a body. The soul is the place that houses your mind, will, and emotions. If you do not strengthen your spirit with the Word of God, then your emotions emerge and begin to work through your bodily members.

Your body is like a car; it will arrive at the destination you have driven it to go. The most important thing about the car is who is behind the wheel. The driver is the one that determines which direction the car will go and how long the car will be driven. This is why it's important to keep your spirit in the driver's seat and not your emotions. Making emotional decisions on the spur of the moment will always yield undesirable results.

What Happens in the Body during Sexual Temptation?

A thought sexual in nature is presented to the mind. You have anywhere from 15 to 30 seconds to do something with that thought. If not, you are willingly allowing your body to prepare for sexual pleasure. Your brain will begin sending signals to the body to release the flow of blood to the genitals. Your penis is a muscle just like any other muscle in your body, but the difference is the amount of nerve endings that are contained within this organ. According to research, there are approximately 4,000 nerve endings in the penis alone.[1] There are hundreds of other nerves that lie within the penal shaft that create intense sensation. Once the blood begins to flow and engorges the penis, causing it to become erect, all of those nerve endings begin sending response signals back to the brain of pleasure.

The reason why I wanted to take out time to discuss this is because like Paul said in Romans 7:23, the war is in your members. With these thousands of nerve endings in your penis that are sending all kind of sensations throughout your body, "is it still possible to shake off the flesh at this point?" Yes, however the temptation just got real.

The best approach to remaining pure is to catch those temptations at the thought level. If you start casting down that imagination at its inception, then you don't have to fight the sensations that will start running through your body once you're aroused. If you aren't watching anything sexual and consistently casting down sexual thoughts, this will eliminate a lot of the temptations that you encounter. This is a MAJOR step in completely getting delivered. You can't wait until you're on fire before you do something. Without an erection, it becomes impossible to masturbate or have sex.

> "And set your minds *and* keep them set on what is above (the higher things), not on the things that are on the earth." Colossians 3:2 (Amplified Bible)

It's just like your digital clock that sits on your nightstand or dresser. When the power goes out, the clock returns to a default of a blinking 12:00 and must be reset. Hebrews 4:12 in the Amplified Bible says that the Word is "full of power." When we disconnect from the power (the Word), our minds return back to the default of being carnal (sinful). Just like the default setting in a clock that blinks at 12:00, when our flesh is acting out with behavior that doesn't glorify God, it's time for a reset. When sexual desires and lustful temptations start coming up to your mind in the form of freaky stuff that you know you've been delivered from, that's your flesh blinking and crying out that it's time to get reset through the Word.

Temptation will always begin with a thought in your mind. You will read this statement over and over throughout the course of this book because this is the foundation for maintaining consistent victory. I cannot stress enough the importance of guarding your thought life. If you would deal with things while they're small, you don't have to worry about a full overgrown situation trying to take you out. A huge mistake that men make is thinking that, "I got this, it's no big deal. Fantasies are harmless because it's not hurting anybody." Please do not be deceived.

Overcome

Chapter 15

How to Set Boundaries for Your Mind

"Finally, brethren, whatsoever things are true, whatsoever things are honest, whatsoever things are just, whatsoever things are pure, whatsoever things are lovely, whatsoever things are of good report; if there be any virtue, and if there be any praise, think on these things." Philippians 4:8

As I was meditating one day, the following revelation came to my heart from this verse. The Apostle Paul was identifying the parameters or boundaries by which our minds were originally designed to operate. There were six categories that he identified by the Holy Spirit. Every thought that we choose to accept and meditate upon should fit into one of these six categories. If not, we are instructed in II Corinthians 10:5 to cast them down. As we renew our minds to the Word of God, these six things create a fence of protection for our soul.

I want you to see these following words as checkpoints: true, honest, just, pure, lovely, and of good report. In the United States, we have border patrol checkpoints between Canada and Mexico. In order for someone from Mexico or Canada to enter our nation, they must provide proper identification. What if the U.S. did not have any border controls, customs, or checkpoints? It would be easy for a terrorist to come in and destroy our country. Likewise, the devil is looking for access into our mind so that he can steal, kill and destroy (John 10:10). If there are no boundaries or checkpoints in your thinking, just imagine the access and ability the enemy has at his disposal. People are not born rapists, pedophiles, and molesters; they started dealing with sexual perversion on a small personal level and never closed their mind off to the devil. As a result, he began to take more and more territory in their soul.

Checkpoints are not instituted to control us as US citizens but it's there for our protection. I have never heard an American say "Hey, let's get rid of all customs, do away with all identification measures (i.e. driver's license, passports, ID) and let us be free." Why? It's because everyone understands the precautionary measures necessary to protect our nation. With this in mind, why do we as believers not take the same approach and sense of precaution for our souls? The Word of God is not here to keep us in bondage or restrict us from enjoying life, but the Father is aware that there is an enemy out there that seeks out our destruction.

"For as he thinketh in his heart,
so is he..." Proverbs 23:7

We must take back our thoughts and not allow the enemy to rob us of freedom. When a thought comes up to the checkpoint of our mind, we must screen it to see if it's of truth, honesty, justice, purity, and kindness. If not, cast it down and refuse it entrance into your heart.

You might say this all sounds real deep and serious. The reason why it sounds deep is because it is deep. Many of you reading this book right now are dealing with strongholds in your flesh because you didn't take your thought life serious enough. Thoughts are very powerful; never underestimate the potential of a thought. Once a thought has been granted access, its main objective is to get planted in your heart. All sexual strongholds started as a thought that turned into a heart's desire. The only way you can truly kill a plant is to destroy the roots. You may have to uproot some things out of your heart that have been planted.

In order to build a boundary or fortress over your thought life, you must take inventory of your current, dominant thoughts. What kind of thoughts are coming to your mind, and how do they line up with or against the Word of God? Take an inventory of what you thought about today. If we were to connect a display cable to your thoughts, would it be safe for us to watch? Just remember the six categories: true, honest, just, pure, lovely, and good report.

Don't Let the Hedge Down

"Hast not thou made an hedge about him, and about his house, and about all that he hath on every side? thou hast blessed the work of his hands, and his substance is increased in the land." Job 1:10

I personally think this is one of the most profound scriptures in the Bible because in this verse satan actually identified a situation that he could not penetrate. As most of you have probably heard the story of Job, satan is coming before God almost whining about how Job is protected on every side. satan was basically saying that he couldn't get to Job regardless of how hard he tried. I think this is pretty amazing if you ask me. In return for Job's obedience to the laws of God, the blessing of the Lord created a hedge or force shield around all that Job possessed. We all know what eventually happened to Job and his family. We have to use deductive reasoning to conclude that somehow this hedge came down, but how?

Let's read Job 3:25, "For the thing which I greatly feared is come upon me, and that which I was afraid of is come unto me." Job allowed fear to weaken the hedge that was there for his protection. Keeping the six categories identified in Philippians 4:8 active in your life is your hedge of protection. The Word of God becomes a force shield and stands guard over your soul. The more you meditate in the Word and resist the enemy, the stronger the hedge of protection becomes in your life. satan is a very crafty spirit so you must pay attention and be alert.

If there is a sex scene in a movie, you should immediately close your eyes or remove yourself from the area. I have heard many men say, "You should be mature enough or spiritually strong enough to handle it." LIES, LIES, LIES! People may not want to believe it but it's wearing down your hedge and diluting your anointing. Just because you may be anointed, it doesn't excuse you from operating in holiness. The anointing on your life was meant for people and the assignments of God, not to solely deal with your own flesh. Paul said I bring under my body, not the anointing, not his apostolic assignment, and not his supernatural revelations. It was Paul's responsibility to keep his body in subjection, and it is your responsibility to do the same.

satan knows he can't take your hedge down. He's no match for the power of God so he has to find a way to get you to let your own hedge down. It's the small foxes that spoil the vine. The little, seemingly insignificant things oftentimes have the most profound effect on your consistent victory. Keep your hedge up! Don't allow anyone to intimidate you because you maintain standards of holiness before God. You will be surprised at how many Christian brothers will tell you it doesn't take all of that but yet they're bound by sexual perversion. Declare this: **I'm not letting my hedge down for one split second!**

Renovate, Restructure, and Reconfigure

In more recent years there has been an extremely high level of home renovation projects. You may have even been a part of a renovation site. Let's take a bathroom renovation for example. Say there is old wallpaper, a moldy tub, rusted faucets and cracked linoleum floors. Now you can do one of two things, you can be cheap and paint over everything with a fresh coat of paint or you can gut out the entire bathroom and create a masterpiece. Most of us have done the first option as it relates to our spiritual lives; we haven't really given ourselves wholly over to God for a complete renovation. We just patch up or paint over what we can to give a nice cosmetic look but underneath the paint we're all cracked up. I wonder how many of you reading this book have everyone thinking that you have it all together in your home, your marriage, on your job, and at church, but deep down inside you're broken, tired, depressed, miserable and at the end of your rope? It's time to deal with those broken pieces in your soul.

Let's first start by taking down the wallpaper. The wallpaper represents what you think about yourself. What do you honestly think about yourself? Just look at your wallpaper, what do you see? Do you see a failure, a screw-up, uneducated, unaccomplished, a loser, a failure, ugly, fat, stupid, no one wants me? You have to come to grips with what you've been looking at when you see yourself because Proverbs 23:7 says, "...as he thinketh in his heart, so is he..." Taking down wallpaper is some serious work especially dependent upon how long it's been up. You must rip down that negative perception about yourself by speaking "I am the righteousness of God in Christ Jesus." I want you to get in front of a mirror and look into your own eyes and say that ten times consecutively, right now.

"For he hath made him to be sin for us, who knew no sin; that we might be made the righteousness of God in him." II Corinthians 5:21

Every time you speak the Word, it not only causes faith to come but it strengthens your spirit and reconfigures your mind. There is a list of scriptures in the back of this book called "freedom confessions" I want you to quote in front of a mirror every morning. The most dominant thoughts in your mind will chart a course for you to follow. You want to head towards God's best for your life.

Old fixtures in a bathroom can represent old ways of doing things. You may need to change how you interact with others. We as men don't like to feel as though we need other people, but life was not meant to be lived solo. God may have someone that can help you in certain areas. It doesn't have to be sin related. You may just need help in your business or your finances. There could be something you're stressing over that may be a cakewalk for someone else. God gave many different gifts and talents to us all so that we can glean from one another, but we as men often struggle unnecessarily because we refuse to allow someone else to help us.

Let go of old foolish instructions from men that never succeeded in life. It's amazing how older men who have jacked up their life want to give you advice on how to make it in this world. Oftentimes I want to ask them, "Well, how did that path work out for you?" Foolish instructions have caused men in this generation to be very jaded and guarded with a skewed perspective on life. You may even have to find a new set of friends because you want to be around individuals that promote your growth and development.

Chapter 16

The Sword of the Spirit Is Your Victory

We have identified and uncovered a variety of topics so far, and I believe it's helping you gain a greater understanding of pitfalls and how to overcome them. In this chapter we will discuss the power to overcome and how to maintain victory through the Word of God. The Word of God is not only a book for encouragement in your walk with Christ; it is also a weapon to use against the enemy and your own flesh. Hebrews 4:12 tell us that the Word is quick and powerful, meaning that it is here to eradicate anything in your life that has no business being there. There is really no sustainable victory without the planting of the Word in your heart. You can avoid temptations through willpower or clever mechanisms, but only the Word can get to the root of that stronghold and bring complete deliverance.

How often are you spending time reading the Word, praying in the Spirit, and worshipping God? It's pretty simple when you think about it because whatever you spend the majority of your time doing will have dominance over you. These three things are key to not only your freedom but your development in Christ. You have to make time for God. Set your alarm and wake up earlier in the day or stay up a little later at night so that you can read your Bible, pray and worship.

God has to become your priority. Could you imagine if you were in a relationship with someone and every time you wanted to see them they had an excuse for why they couldn't spend time with you? What would you think after a while? You would think that they weren't interested in you. Where would we all be if God stopped being interested in us?

The Word of God was written with the intent and purpose that God and His ways would be revealed to us so that we might become like Him. When we got born-again we became a new creature in Christ (II Corinthians 5:17). Salvation is instant but spiritual development takes time. Our spirit man must be developed through spending time in the Word of God. It's just like bringing a newborn baby home from the hospital and expecting them to clothe, feed, and wash themselves. These things take time through training and development to bring a child to the place where they can master these things. Our time in the Word is a time of development and training in how to live according to the kingdom's way of operating. However, if we fail to understand the purpose for the Word then we miss out on the benefits that it produces.

"All scripture is given by inspiration of God, and is profitable for doctrine, for reproof, for correction, for instruction in righteousness." II Timothy 3:16

There are four major categories or areas through which the Word benefits us as a believer: it shapes our faith (doctrine); it analyzes and exposes error (reproof); it adjusts and realigns actions (correction); and it gives advice or counsel (instruction). God has breathed a scripture that fits into one of these four categories that carries the power to bring about deliverance and change.

Hebrews 4:12 (Amplified Bible) reminds us, "For the Word that God speaks is alive and full of power [making it active, operative, energizing, and effective]..." Every word that proceeds out of God carries the potential to be a reality in your life, but it is solely based upon you. Something that carries potential means that it is "capable of being or becoming; having latent ability."[1] Now, if dwelling on the inside of you is the same spirit that raised Christ from the dead, you have the potential of being just like Christ.

It is not enough to know that we have the potential to walk like Christ and be full of the Holy Ghost and power. We must take it a step further and manifest this power in our lives. Brother Kenneth E. Hagin once said that sometimes we're looking for the spectacular and miss the supernatural. Living in holiness and sanctification is supernatural.

Meditation

One way we unlock the power of the Word is through meditation. The freedom confessions in the back of this book are scriptures that I want you to start meditating on every day. Those scriptures help identify who you are, what has been provided for you, and what your life should look like. If you read through those scriptures and your life doesn't look like what God said, it's time to meditate on that scripture until revelation comes on how to make that adjustment.

Let's take one of the scriptures as an example, and I'll show you how to meditate. James 4:7 says, "Submit yourselves therefore to God. Resist the devil, and he will flee from you." You first start in meditation by dissecting what is being said piece by piece. Just like you don't put a whole steak in your mouth at one time but cut one piece at a time and chew, meditation is the same. Meditation is like chewing. The first two words of this scripture is a piece, "submit yourselves." Don't always assume you know what a word means, so let's look up what it means to submit. The word *submit* means to "give over or yield to the power or authority of another; to obey."[2] Now, start chewing on this definition.

You chew by examining your life based on this word submit. Have I been yielding and giving over to the authority of God? Has God asked me to do something that I haven't done yet? God has been dealing with me about forgiving someone, have I done it? You continue this process through the entire verse. After you have completed your meditation, then it's time to pray and make adjustments. If your answer to some of the questions you asked yourself were not right then you need to repent. Ask the Father to forgive you for missing the mark. Repent for not obeying what you know to do is right. Once you repent, now it's time to turn to the Holy Spirit and ask Him to help you make this turn in the right direction.

Meditating in the Word is not a once a week regimen. It must be done continuously every day so that the Word is planted in your heart. If we don't continue to plant the Word in our heart, it can slip away from us and cause our faith to become weak. Have you ever had someone ask you about a certain scripture, but you couldn't remember what it said? This is a sign that the Word which was once in your heart has slipped away. All you have to do is go back to those scriptures and begin to read and meditate them once again.

It becomes easier to let the Word slip in areas you already know because you stopped meditating. There are some scenarios where the Spirit of God will not speak anything new until you go back and obey the first set of instructions that were given.

> "My son, attend to my words; incline thine
> ear unto my sayings. Let them not depart
> from thine eyes; keep them in the midst
> of thine heart." Proverbs 4:20-21

In verse 21, Solomon mentioned an important aspect of meditation that we often take for granted which is keeping the Word before our eyes. Many times the reason we take it for granted is because we may have memorized a scripture or heard it hundreds of times. You may hear believers say, "Oh, I already know that scripture." A fresh planting and watering of the Word comes when we read the Word with our eyes. Solomon said "don't let it depart." He wouldn't have said it if it wasn't possible to depart.

The number one way the Word departs from our eyes is by allowing ourselves to get too busy. We get so caught up in the affairs of life that by the time we find a free moment the last thing we want to do is read the Word. Make a practice of going back to scriptures you already know and reading them again. The Holy Spirit will breathe fresh revelation on that scripture you may have known for many years.

The Holy Spirit

One of the functions of the Holy Spirit is to take the Word and show us things in our life that may need correcting or help us in areas where we may be completely ignorant. He will always speak in line with the Word of God. You will never be led by the Holy

Ghost apart from the Word. John 16:13 tells us that the Holy Spirit will guide us into all truth.

We need to know the truth about our situations. Why am I still dealing with this issue? Where have I opened the door to the enemy? How do I close the door on this thing? The Holy Spirit is here to help us.

If you pay attention you can recognize the Holy Spirit's prompting before you sin. There is an inner nudging within you that you don't need to do something, or you may sense that you don't need to go somewhere. Sometimes we override this prompting and allow our flesh to override that warning. At the end of the day you shake your head because a lot of things that you've endured could've been avoided if only you had listened to the Holy Spirit.

The Sword

"For the word of God is quick, and powerful, and sharper than any twoedged sword, piercing even to the dividing asunder of soul and spirit, and of the joints and marrow, and is a discerner of the thoughts and intents of the heart." Hebrews 4:12

The Word of God has self-contained power which gives it efficacy or the ability to produce a desired result without help. There is a word in the Bible that has enough power to change you and any situation in your life forever. Think of scriptures as explosive material like dynamite or C4. This power is able to transform hearts and minds, deliver from habits and addictions, bring peace, and even eradicate lack. However, just like a bomb, it doesn't matter how powerful it may be if there isn't a detonator to trigger the explosion.

The Word of God must be activated in order for it to work. Our faith is the trigger switch that releases the power that lies within the Word. You activate the Word by believing and confessing it over your life.

Chapter 17

Jesus' Blood Still Works

I am seeing amongst believers a great lack of understanding of what Jesus' blood represents in our life today. We're going to discuss in this chapter why Jesus died and the significance of His blood being shed.

Blood Covenant

As we read in the Old Testament, one of the most powerful ways to make covenant was through the shedding of blood. The blood covenant was a binding agreement among two people who would cut themselves and mix their blood together. This represented that nothing but death would separate them from fulfilling their part of the agreement. Even in marriage during intercourse a virgin's hymen is broken, and the blood is shed on the man to consummate the covenant of marriage. They are both coming together in a blood covenant to uphold their responsibilities to care, nourish, protect, and love each other until death.

Blood is also a symbol of purchase or to pardon a transgression. When Adam sinned in the Garden of Eden, an animal was killed and God took the skin of the animal and clothed Adam and Eve according to Genesis 3:21. This was symbolic of Jesus being sacrificed for the sins of mankind and because of His sacrifice we are clothed with a garment of righteousness.

Resisting the Enemy

"Rebuke the devil" or "plead the blood" are terms you've probably heard used in church, but what does it mean? To rebuke simply means to resist, and to plead means to withstand. When you rebuke the enemy, you are resisting him or blocking him from you. The way you resist the devil is through the Word of God. In Luke Chapter 4 when Jesus was tempted in the wilderness, He responded with a scripture (it is written) to every temptation. This is a great example of how we ought to rebuke or resist satan.

The way the devil comes to us is through our thoughts. He wants us to respond to that thought in a way that is against the Bible because it gives him access in our lives to wreak havoc. When a thought comes to your mind that you know is not according to the Word and it is not true, honest, just, pure, and lovely (Philippians 4:8) you can open your mouth boldly and say:

> No devil, I refuse to allow that thought to dwell in my mind. I resist you spirit of perversion. You will not have access to my soul. I plead the blood of Jesus over my mind. I cast down every thought, every imagination, and every fantasy that tries to exalt itself above the truth of the Word. I only think on what is pure and holy, and I have soundness of mind in Jesus' name.

Use this confession in your daily life to keep negative thoughts from resting in your mind. An old wise tale says, "you can't stop a bird from flying over your head, but you can stop it from building a nest there."

Now, I'm not going to tell you that this will be easy. There will be times where you might have to confess the Word all day long. You must understand the devil can put up a good fight, but you have been given authority to break his power with the Word (Luke 10:19). Depending upon how long you've been allowing lustful images or fantasies to dwell in your thinking, it may take some time to tear down these strongholds.

Regardless, glory be to God for the Word and the blood of Jesus that works every time.

I want to talk a little more about 'pleading the blood of Jesus.' Most people don't really know how to use this powerful weapon in the Spirit and oftentimes have misunderstood its function. In recent years, there are some religious groups that have taken the hymnals that mention the blood out of the song books. There's this saying that I have, "whatever you don't understand you won't value, whatever you don't value you won't spend time with, and whatever you don't spend time with, you won't see the fruit of it." We as the Church have not been taught in more recent years about what the blood did for us, is currently doing, and what it will continue to do on our behalf. People will disregard what they don't understand.

"...for the accuser of our brethren is cast down, which accused them before our God day and night. And they overcame him by the blood of the Lamb, and by the word of their testimony; and they loved not their lives unto the death." Revelation 12:10-11

Take a good look at this phrase, "And they overcame him by the blood of the Lamb..." If you look at the previous verse, you'll see that the "him" is referring to satan (accuser of the brethren). Notice, they overcame him by the blood. The blood of Jesus is a weapon of defense against the enemy. satan cannot oppose the blood. When Jesus died and went to hell, He arose on the third day by the glory of God taking back authority and dominion (Romans 6:4).

The same blood that washed you from your sins was sprinkled on the mercy seat in Heaven and still speaks on your behalf. In other words, the blood that Jesus shed on the cross still has the same power. It still cleanses, redeems, sanctifies, and protects. It has never diminished its ability to liberate mankind from the works of darkness. Jesus' blood lives forever. Hebrews 10:19 says, "Having therefore, brethren, boldness to enter into the holiest by the blood of Jesus." The blood of Jesus also made us righteous and purified our hearts. It gives us access to enter into the very presence of God without a sense of guilt or shame.

Now let's go a little deeper in this study about the blood. You can also apply the blood to every area of your life by "pleading the blood." The word *plead* is mainly used in more of a legal setting in which a defendant will respond to a charge that has been filed against him. The dictionary definition means "to provide an argument or appeal; to declare oneself to be (guilty or not guilty) in answer to the charge; to use arguments or persuasions, as with a person, for or against something."[1]

When you say, "I plead the blood of Jesus," you are declaring that you are under the dominion of Jesus and claiming that this area is off limits to the devil. Jesus shed His blood so that we could walk in liberty. Pornography, masturbation, and sex does not have dominion over you. Declare every day that your mind has been freed because of the blood of Jesus.

The enemy will come to challenge your freedom because he wants you back in bondage. satan will never be satisfied until everything pertaining to you is utterly destroyed. This is why you cannot afford to play around with sexual perversion because he's waiting on an entrance in your life. Stop giving the devil an opportunity! You don't have to worry about fighting evil temptations when you release the power of the blood which fights for you.

"Therefore thus saith the Lord; Behold, I
will plead thy cause, and take vengeance
for thee..." Jeremiah 51:36

Thank God we don't have to do this on our own! If God is for us, who can be against us? You are a part of the family of God. You are His beloved son, and there is nothing that your Father would not do for you. It brings the Father so much pain when He sees His children trapped in pitfalls and snares set up by the enemy. He is standing with His hands reached out to you, but you must reach back and take hold of Him. God is not bothered by the devil in the least bit. He's concerned about you.

"For whosoever shall call upon the name of
the Lord shall be saved." Romans 10:13

A child has a right to call on their parent at any moment, and the parent would naturally respond with care and concern. However, a child that does not belong to the parent does not have the same privileges as the one who does belong. You have a right to exercise authority through the name of Jesus, you he HHave a right to plead the blood of Jesus, and you have a right to use the Word of God as a weapon. This is what it means to be a part of the family of God. God takes up your cause and fights on your behalf because you are His child. He didn't just save us and leave us helpless to fend for ourselves. He gave us the power to live victoriously.

Chapter 18

Watchman over
Your Gates

Man was created as a triune being: he is a spirit, possesses a soul, and lives in a body. Just like the physical body receives nourishment through consuming food, the spirit of man is nourished through three gates. These three gates to your spirit are: your eyes, ears and mouth. The reason we call them gates is because a gate has the ability to allow something in or keep it out. Whatever is deposited in your spirit is a result of you opening one of your gates and allowing it in your life.

The Bible gives many references and similitude to the watchman of a city. A watchman was a person that was typically set at the corners of the city wall; one man for each direction (north, south, east, west). The job required that they work in shifts or "watches" which were in three hour increments. Their primary function was to stand guard and see if an enemy was coming from afar or when merchants would come to bring trade to the city. At their command, the porter (gate opener) would open or close the city gates.

The watchman would also blow the trumpet for battle if an enemy was seen approaching. One profound thing about how they would engage their enemy is that they would go out to meet the enemy. This protected the city by not allowing the enemy to get close. If a watchman failed to see the enemy and allowed them to storm the gates or climb over the city walls, the likelihood of that city winning was impossible. The city wall was the people's greatest defense against attack.

> "But know this, that if the goodman of the house had known in what watch the thief would come, he would have watched, and would not have suffered his house to be broken up." Matthew 24:43

In this passage of scripture, Jesus was taking the analogy of a watchman and the city to relate it to our personal lives. Jesus was relating this to how we should keep watch over our lives and not allow the thief (devil) to attack us unawares. We must remain watchful with our spiritual eyes to see when the enemy is coming afar off. When you start noticing small things or random thoughts of sexual perversion, this is a cue to get your weapons ready for the battle.

Don't Ignore the Watchman

You can almost sense when the enemy is about to bring some foolishness your way. It's almost like an inner prompting that your watchman (your spirit) is seeing that an attack is coming. This is why it is imperative that you stay full of the Word, in the presence of God, and around other strong believers because you want your watchman to be agile and fit, not fat and lazy. When it's show time, you want your watchman on duty and ready with a sword (Word of God) in his hand.

Stop ignoring or overriding that inner prompting! If you agree to admit, in the past right before you've missed the mark, there was something on the inside that was telling you "*don't watch that, don't go there, walk away from it, leave now, stop playing around with that.*" When you hear those things, this is your watchman blowing the trumpet, sounding the alarm. He's speaking to your porter (your will), "don't open the gate, don't let it in, don't let it destroy the city." Many painful and tragic situations could've been avoided if we would've taken more time to pay attention to our watchman.

Training Your Watchman

A person does not become unhealthy by simply thinking about cheeseburgers, French fries, pizzas, etc. They became that way by what they have consumed in abundance. This individual would have never acquired an appetite for unhealthy foods if they would've never experimented with this type of food. The same is true concerning our spirit man. What have we allowed our eyes to watch on TV, Internet and movies? What conversations have we heard or allowed ourselves to be a part of? What have we let come out of our mouth? Those are the things that begin to shape our spirit.

This is how the battle begins! Yes, the enemy will try to bring thoughts, imaginations and fantasies to your mind, but sometimes he's using tools that we have given him. When we expose our soul to sin, the enemy has something to use against us. Have you noticed that you don't think about something until you're exposed to it? As an adult that has graduated from college, I don't sit up thinking about calculus. Why? Because it was never a part of my course study. My mind can only rehearse what I've had contact with in the past. Even with things that I did study in my undergraduate studies such as Accounting 1 and 2, I vaguely remember it because I've stayed away from it for so long.

You must train your spirit by monitoring your gates. As you control the content that is received through your eyes, ears and mouth, you're shaping your spirit man. When we allow our flesh to run wild, we exhibit a lack of discipline. It takes discipline to meditate the Word and pray in the Spirit.

I'm sure we have all witnessed a young toddler in the store having a tantrum. What is the first thing that usually comes to your mind when you see this? You're probably thinking that the parent has not taught the child discipline and obedience. It's the same way the Father is watching you. He's looking at your spirit and wondering why you have not disciplined your flesh. Paul said in I Corinthians 9:27, "But I keep under my body, and bring it into subjection..." God is not going to keep your body. You're responsible for keeping your body. God is only responsible for keeping His Word.

Take baby steps and disconnect from either movies or television for two weeks. Watch how your spirit will begin to detox, and your mind will settle down. You don't even have to spend an extreme amount of time in the Word and prayer, but the time you do spend will stick to your heart. You won't lose it so easily. Whatever you spend the abundance of your time in will be the very thing that will anchor down in your spirit.

"And the cares of this world, and the deceitfulness of riches, and the lusts of other things entering in, **choke the word**, and it becometh unfruitful." Mark 4:19 (emphasis added)

Notice what these things do to the Word of God that you are trying to plant in your heart. It "chokes the word." Most of the things on television and in the movies are sinful, lustful things that most Christians don't partake of in their personal lives. Therefore, Christians shouldn't allow these things to be a source of entertainment. The word *choke* means: "to stop by or as if by strangling or stifling; to become obstructed, clogged, or otherwise stopped; to block."[1]

In the Greek language the word choke is "sumpnigo" which means to strangle completely, to drown, to crowd.[2] satan throws these things our way so that the Word never takes root in our heart. Of course there will be some people who will try to get legalistic and ask how many hours they should watch television, movies, or be on the Internet. It will be different for each person depending upon what they may be watching. However, a safe guide is that you don't spend more time with things of this world than you do in the Word and prayer. Keep a guard over your gates!

Chapter 19

The 3 Fears: Falling, Failing & Faltering

As you begin to walk in the truth of the Word of God that has been outlined in this book, the enemy will try to come at you from a totally different angle than what you might expect. Fear will paralyze you from moving forward. It is an immobilizer. I want to discuss three fears that will meet you on your road to overcoming:

1. The fear of not being able to maintain your freedom
2. The fear of letting God down
3. The fear of not making it into Heaven

Fear 1: Not Maintaining My Freedom

I found myself standing face-to-face with this fear several years ago. To give you a brief background of my life, I was raised in the home of a minister and for the most part overcame most of the pitfalls that teenagers go through (all Glory to God). I then went off to college, graduated, and got out on my own with no major hiccups.

One day around the age of 23, this fear of not being able to maintain my witness for Christ started attacking my mind. I started noticing friends around me compromise in the area of sexual purity, and the enemy would tell me that I was next. For a second I started feeling hopeless, like maybe there was no way to remain pure before the Lord living in this society. I mean you can't even go shopping without seeing images of half naked women with their boobs staring you in the face. How does God expect us to remain pure while living in a sexually charged society? I remember clear as day the Holy Spirit speaking up in my spirit, "now unto Him that is able to keep you from falling." I looked it up in the Amplified Bible and it reads:

> "Now to Him Who is able to keep you without stumbling *or* slipping *or* falling, and to present [you] unblemished (blameless and faultless) before the presence of His glory in triumphant joy *and* exultation [with unspeakable, ecstatic delight]" Jude 24 (Amplified Bible)

The more I began to meditate on this scripture, the more confident I became. I took this as my promise from the Lord that if I remained connected to the true vine (John 15) that He would become my keeper. In the Pentecostal denomination they refer to God as a "keeper" and that, "He'll keep you if you want to be kept." I remember hearing Kenneth E. Hagin say many times, "The only way that I'm going down is if the Word goes down, and if the Word isn't going down then I'm not going down." The more and more I kept confessing these things, faith started rising up in my heart and I began to boldly attack that spirit of fear. Romans 10:17 tells us that "...faith cometh by hearing, and hearing by the word of God." Make this confession:

> Father, according to Isaiah 55:11, you said that your Word would not return void, so I send forth your Word and release my faith today that you are able to keep me from stumbling, slipping, or falling into any area of sexual immorality. I give myself over to your care. I refuse to allow fear to reign over me. Fear doesn't come from you Father, and I don't accept it (II Timothy 1:7). I know you love me and only want the best for me and will do anything for me, so I hang my

confidence on your Word and not on how I feel in Jesus' Name, Amen.

Fear 2: Letting God Down

This is the fear that hits the jugular vein; it hurts the most. satan is a pretty cruel individual because he knows how much you love God and want to live right. He will use your sins against you to make you feel worthless and that God doesn't want you. One thing you must always remain convinced of is God's indescribable love for you. I'm telling you there is no person or thing in this world that loves you more than God.

> "He that loveth not knoweth not God; for God is love. In this was manifested the love of God toward us, because that God sent his only begotten Son into the world, that we might live through him. Herein is love, not that we loved God, but that he loved us, and sent his Son to be the propitiation for our sins." I John 4:8-10

At the end of this chapter I am going to list some scriptures on the Father's love for you so you can finally once and for all lay down this feeling of unworthiness. It can be shame from your past, something you're currently dealing with, or unclean desires that you don't want anyone to know about. When you become perfected in the love of God, it casts out all fear.

"There is no fear in love; but perfect love casteth out fear: because fear hath torment. He that feareth is not made perfect in love." I John 4:18

If you do happen to fall, dust yourself off and keep going after God. I think the biggest mistake that we as believers make is giving up on God because we feel like we've disappointed Him. It's funny how we limit God to human emotions and feelings or what we would do in a certain situation. Thank God He isn't like us (man). He loves us unconditionally according to Lamentations 3:22-23. Make this promise between you and God:

Regardless of what happens in my life, I will forever be chasing after more of God. I will not give up on my relationship with the Father because of past mistakes. His mercies are new to me every morning, and I wake up with a fresh start.

Fear 3: Not Making It into Heaven

Heaven is our eternal home. We as believers are only pilgrims passing through this life making our voyage home. In Philippians 1:23, Paul said, "For I am in a strait between two, having a desire to depart, and to be with Christ; which is far better." Heaven is a real place, and the real you (your spirit) longs to be there with God. Our ultimate destination when our spirit leaves this body is to be with Christ (II Corinthians 5:8).

When Paul wrote in Galatians 5:19-21 about those that practice sin "shall not inherit the kingdom of God," he did not write this to produce a spirit of fear but to instill a respect and reverence for God's holiness. When God created man, He created him with the freedom to choose. God doesn't force us through manipulation and fear. It is the goodness of God that leads a person to repentance (Romans 2:4); however, we can't allow God's grace and mercy to be trampled upon by the appetite of our flesh (Hebrews 10:26-30).

> "But I keep under my body, and bring it into
> subjection: lest that by any means, when
> I have preached to others, I myself should
> be a castaway." I Corinthians 9:27

You might ask, "What is the middle of the road on this subject?" You don't want to fall on either side of the ditch: fear of not being good enough to go to Heaven or abusing the grace of God and practicing sin. The proper balance is to accept what Christ has already done for you on the cross and continue to walk in that revelation.

> "Who hath delivered us from the power of darkness, and hath translated us into the kingdom of his dear Son: In whom we have redemption through his blood, even the forgiveness of sins:" Colossians 1:13-14

Notice what Paul revealed in these verses, Christ has already delivered and redeemed us through His blood. It's our spirit that has been redeemed and delivered, not our soul or body. Our soul must be transformed, and our body must be reprogrammed. We already talked about in previous chapters how to renew our soul (mind, will, and emotions) and keep our body under. You may have to rehearse some of these chapters over and over until they become a revelation to you.

I have heard so many people make this famous statement, "How can a person commit a sin if they're supposed to be a Christian?" The real person on the inside didn't commit the sin, it's the flesh nature that has not been delivered through the Word of God that has led the individual into sin.

Resist the fear of sin! Confess this over yourself:

> I speak to the spirit of fear that wants to hold me captive. I don't walk in fear of sin. I have been delivered through the blood of Jesus. I hold the blood of Jesus over my thoughts, over my heart, over my will, and over my body. I am controlled by the Holy Ghost and not my feelings. I fear not. I refuse to fear. I won't fear. I walk in the spirit of life which is in Christ Jesus. I have been made free.

Chapter 20

I Am the Man That God Is Looking For

The very reason why I wrote this book is to remind you of who you are in Christ and help you to not disqualify yourself from the race that God has set before you. God created you with a purpose that only you can fulfill. The enemy would love nothing more than to keep men in bondage so they never bring freedom to anyone else. The devil doesn't mind you going to Heaven. He just doesn't want you to take anyone with you. He doesn't want your life to reflect the goodness of God which will lead others to repentance.

Side Note: We are all called to evangelize and win the lost; however, DO NOT, and I repeat DO NOT spend time discipling a female. You can lead her to Christ but you need to quickly refer her to another sister in the Lord to help develop her in the things of God. It is very easy to become emotionally involved with a new convert. They can begin to latch on to the God in you and become infatuated with your spiritual maturity. There are several men that I know who have wrecked their lives getting hooked up with a baby Christian.

As Christian men we can sometimes get too focused on the temptation in our lives. Follow the things that we have outlined in this book, but don't allow the enemy to steal your focus. The enemy will use whatever you may be attracted to in your flesh to lure your attention away from your purpose. Anything that comes into your life that is not assisting you is potentially resisting your purpose.

According to dictionary.com, the word *distraction* is defined as "an interruption; an obstacle to concentration."[1] Distractions are demonic interruptions sent to derail you. The longer you stay distracted, the more frustrated you'll become because your focus has been broken. Frustration then turns into spiritual depression where you begin to doubt if God loves you or if He can still use you. This state of mind will eventually lead to denial if you don't get your mind renewed.

Denial presents a very dangerous attitude where you begin to feel a myriad of emotions: this is just who I am; I've gone too far; there's no hope left for me; it's somebody else's fault; I can never be free. Distractions lead to frustration, frustration leads to depression, and depression leads to denial.

We all know the story of Adam and Eve and how they ate of the fruit in the Garden of Eden of which the Lord told them not to partake of. I want to look at this story in a completely different context.

> "And when the woman saw that the tree was good
> for food, and that it was pleasant to the eyes, and
> a tree to be desired to make one wise, she took of
> the fruit thereof, and did eat, and gave also unto
> her husband with her; and he did eat." Genesis 3:6

I want you to take note of the phrase, "and when the woman saw..." We know that Adam and Even weren't blind so this could not have been the first time they saw the fruit on this tree, but I submit to you this was the first time the fruit caught the attention of their flesh and they became distracted.

Let's look at how this cycle of distraction happened in Adam.

- Distraction: Adam ate the fruit.
- Frustration: Adam is now naked, so he sewed fig leaves to cover himself.
- Depression: The condemnation that Adam felt when he heard God's voice.
- Denial: Adam blamed Eve for why he transgressed against God.

Notice what being distracted cost Adam. He lost his position, his power, and his prominence. Be watchful of the things that keep you distracted because those distractions will eventually cost you the glory!

God is so merciful and gracious because even though God was aware that Adam had sinned, He still came looking for him. God didn't come down with wrath and anger ready to kill him. All God wanted to know is, "where art thou?" Isn't it amazing that even when we mess up, God still comes looking for us?

When God realized that Adam hadn't showed up in the meeting place where they would normally commune, He began searching for him. Why has Adam left his post? This was probably the first time Adam had ever missed his appointment with Jehovah. We are in a season now where God is coming to visit the body of Christ. Will He find you awaiting His visitation, or will you be hiding in the bushes?

The devil's main objective after we miss the mark is to make sure we hide from the presence of the Lord. Now, I can't say this for certain but I would like to believe that if Adam would have cried out to the Father after he sinned and asked for His mercy that God would have forgiven him. Instead Adam allowed the distraction to lead him to frustration, depression, and denial.

God is calling you today. He's wondering why you have not come into His presence. Are you hiding in the bushes like Adam or are you ready to answer the Lord "Here am I" (Isaiah 6:8)? You might have to come nasty and dirty, filthy and messed up, but come anyway. That's all that God has been waiting on from you - for you to simply show up to meet with Him. When you get a revelation that YOU ARE the man that God has been looking for, you will refuse to let anything distract you.

I leave you with this thought…as you wake up in the morning getting ready to head to work, you understand that you have a window of time to get prepared and ready to walk out the door. If a salesman or a Jehovah Witness came knocking at your door while you were trying to get ready for work, your disposition would be firm that you really didn't have time to talk because you're on your way to work. If somebody called you while you were getting dressed you might have to tell them to call you back because you're getting ready for work. You realize that distractions during this time could potentially cause you to be late for work, and if you're late too many times you might not have a job. You understand that your livelihood is on the line.

The moral of this example is to not be late for your appointment with destiny. God has something great in store for you, and you can't afford to allow sexual sin to keep you distracted. When distractions come knocking at your door, just remember you're on your way somewhere in God, and you can't afford to be late.

Chapter 21

For Ministers of
the Gospel

I want you to carefully read the section towards the
end of Chapter 15 entitled "Don't Let the Hedge Down."
As a minister of the Gospel, I am grievously concerned
because I am seeing this great deception coming upon
some who are anointed. Some think just because the
anointing is flowing in their life and people are getting
healed, delivered and set free under their ministry
that they don't have to uphold a standard of holiness
before the Lord. Don't let the anointing on your life
fool you. If you are in any kind of sexual sin, this is
your warning from the Lord that it's time to get right.

In recent times we have been hearing a lot on the
subject of grace which has caused the Church to lull
to sleep. We are not as vigilant on holiness and upright
living as we used to be in the past. Many are labeling

those that bring correction to sin as being judgmental and critical.

When did we become so indifferent to sin? I don't want you to think about other Christians that you know of right now that are in sin. I want you to examine your own life. Have you started making allowances for sin in your life? It's so easy to preach to someone else, to counsel someone else, to pray for someone else, but let's take a minute and see if you are the one that needs to receive ministry.

We are all very familiar with the story of Samson. Some of you have probably preached from this text many times. Every time I hear the end of the story, I always do a self-reflection. Samson's downfall was not specifically Delilah, it was the fact that he didn't address the sin because it didn't seem to affect his anointing at first. For a good while he was able to have his cake and eat his ice cream too. It wasn't until one day when Samson went to shake himself and didn't realize the Lord had departed. Judges 16:20 says, "... And he awoke out of his sleep, and said, I will go out as at other times before, and shake myself. And he wist not that the Lord was departed from him."

This is why I said at the beginning of this chapter, "don't let the anointing fool you." You can be going, moving and shaking with power and not realize your anointing is slipping away from you. If you miss the mark, the anointing will not automatically leave you right away. This can be very deceiving for some so instead of getting right and staying away from immorality, they continue down that road of sin. Grace is available for you to make the turn, to get it right, and to repent. It's almost like walking across a frozen lake in the winter. It's easier for water to freeze and become solid when it's shallow because there's not much depth, but when you start getting in the middle of the lake it becomes harder to support your weight.

I know your mind is probably turning and thinking that no one is perfect and as long as we are in this body the flesh will tend to act up sometimes. I understand but hear what I'm saying. It's much easier to pull yourself back on the banks when you're in shallow water then it is if you fall in the middle of the lake.

Grace is what's holding you up, but the further you get out in sin the less grace can be applied because you're abusing the grace upon your life. There will come a point where grace can no longer uphold the weight of your sin and judgment will fall. We have seen way too many ministers exposed in the news that kept going and never turned around. Don't let this be you.

The Lord is full of mercy and compassion, but please do not take God or the things of God for a joke. When the hand of the Lord is removed from you, what can you do? Genesis 6:3 says, "And the Lord said, My spirit shall not always strive with man..."

As soon as you miss the mark, you need to acknowledge it, get in the Word, and call a close brother that can keep you accountable. You are very useful to God. He gave you gifts, talents, anointings and graces that everyone doesn't possess. There are many people that would love to operate in the power that is upon your life. Don't take it for granted. You have to realize that what God has imparted to you is valuable and must be protected. Guard the anointing and keep it safe. The devil would love nothing more than to strip you of the very thing that defeats him.

We have much work to do for God, and we need all hands on deck. The body of Christ has need of you to take your place. I'm rooting for you and your ministry. God bless!

Resources

Freedom Confessions

Jesus offered Himself without spot to God, and through His blood my conscience has been purged from dead works to serve the living God. – Hebrews 9:14

I have redemption through His blood, the forgiveness of sins, according to the riches of His grace. – Ephesians 1:7

I come boldly to the throne of grace that I may obtain mercy today, and I receive grace to help me in my time of need. – Hebrews 4:16

I have been delivered from the power of darkness and translated into the Kingdom of God; in whom I have redemption through His blood the forgiveness of my sins. – Colossians 1:13-14

I submit myself to God. I resist the devil and he flees from me. – James 4:7

I have been given authority over all the power of the enemy, and nothing shall hurt (trap, snare, trick, or bind) me. – Luke 10:19

I have been sanctified by the blood of Jesus. – Hebrews 13:12

Jesus, you have redeemed me to God by your precious blood. – Revelation 5:9

I have been washed from my sins in His own blood. – Revelation 1:5

Christ purchased my freedom and redeemed me from the curse of the law and its condemnation. – Galatians 3:13 (Amplified Bible)

I have overcome the enemy and all of his tactics by the blood of the Lamb and the word of my testimony. – Revelations 12:11

I am no longer under condemnation because I am in Christ Jesus. For the law of the Spirit of life in Christ Jesus has made me free from the law of sin and death. – Romans 8:1-2

Jesus was made sin for me that I might be made the righteousness of God in Him. – II Corinthians 5:21

In all things I am more than a conqueror and gain a surpassing victory through Christ who loves me. – Romans 8:37 (Amplified Bible)

I am crucified with Christ. Nevertheless I live; yet not I, but Christ lives in me. And the life which I now live in the flesh, I live by the faith of the Son of God who loved me and gave Himself for me. – Galatians 2:20

I delight to do your will, O my God, for your laws are within my heart. – Psalm 40:8

I am renewed in the spirit of my mind, and I put on the new man that is like God created in righteousness and true holiness. – Ephesians 4:23-24

I make a choice to think on things that are true, honest, just, pure and lovely. – Philippians 4:8

I have been given the mind of Christ. – I Corinthians 2:16

With my mind I serve the law of God. – Romans 7:25

I set my mind and keep it set on the things above, not on the things on the earth. I set my mind on the things of God. – Colossians 3:2

Because I trust in you Lord, You will keep my mind in perfect peace because I focus on thee. – Isaiah 26:3

I cast down imaginations, fantasies, thoughts, and every high thing that tries to exalt itself above the truth of God, and I bring it into captivity to the obedience of Christ – II Corinthians 10:5

I am not conformed to this world's way of thinking but I am transformed by the renewing of my mind, that I may prove what is that good and acceptable and perfect will of God. – Romans 12:2

I walk in the spirit and I do not fulfill or indulge in the lust of the flesh – Galatians 5:16

I have overcome because greater is He that is in me than he that is in the world – I John 4:4

No temptation has taken me but such as is common to man. God is faithful who will not suffer me to be tempted above that which I am able to endure. He will, with the temptation, also make a way of escape, that I may be able to bear it. – I Corinthians 10:13

Love Confession

I Corinthians 13:4-8

I endure long and am patient and kind with_____; I am never envious nor boil over with jealousy. I am not boastful or vainglorious and do not display myself haughtily with _____. I am not conceited arrogant or inflated with pride. I am not rude unmannerly and do not act unbecomingly with _____. God's love in me does not insist on its own rights or its own way, for I am not self-seeking, touchy, fretful or resentful towards _____. I take no account of the evil done to me nor do I pay attention to the suffered wrong by _____. I do not rejoice at injustice and unrighteousness, but rejoice when right and truth prevail. I bear up under anything and everything that comes, and I am ever ready to believe the best of _____. My hopes are fadeless under all circumstances, and I endure everything without weakening. My love never fails, never fades out, becomes obsolete or comes to an end with _____.

God's Love towards Me

He that hath my commandments, and keepeth them, he it is that loveth me: and he that loveth me shall be loved of my Father, and I will love him, and will manifest myself to him. - John 14:21

As the Father hath loved me, so have I loved you: continue ye in my love. - John 15:9

This is my commandment, That ye love one another, as I have loved you. - John 15:12

For the Father himself loveth you, because ye have loved me, and have believed that I came out from God. - John 16:27

But God commendeth his love toward us, in that, while we were yet sinners, Christ died for us. - Romans 5:8

Who shall separate us from the love of Christ? shall tribulation, or distress, or persecution, or famine, or nakedness, or peril, or sword? - Romans 8:35

Nay, in all these things we are more than conquerors through him that loved us. - Romans 8:37

Nor height, nor depth, nor any other creature, shall be able to separate us from the love of God, which is in Christ Jesus our Lord. - Romans 8:39

But God, who is rich in mercy, for his great love wherewith he loved us, - Ephesians 2:4

And walk in love, as Christ also hath loved us, and hath given himself for us an offering and a sacrifice to God for a sweet smelling savour. - Ephesians 5:2

Now our Lord Jesus Christ himself, and God, even our Father, which hath loved us, and hath given us everlasting consolation and good hope through grace, - II Thessalonians 2:16

Behold, what manner of love the Father hath bestowed upon us, that we should be called the sons of God: therefore the world knoweth us not, because it knew him not. – I John 3:1

In this was manifested the love of God toward us, because that God sent his only begotten Son into the world, that we might live through him. – I John 4:9

Herein is love, not that we loved God, but that he loved us, and sent his Son to be the propitiation for our sins. – I John 4:10

We love him, because he first loved us. – I John 4:19

And from Jesus Christ, who is the faithful witness, and the first begotten of the dead, and the prince of the kings of the earth. Unto him that loved us, and washed us from our sins in his own blood, - Revelation 1:5

As many as I love, I rebuke and chasten: be zealous therefore, and repent. – Revelation 3:19

I am… Confessions

I am a mighty man of valor, and the strength of God goes before me.

I am equipped for every challenge, test, trial or obstacle that comes my way.

I am full of the wisdom of God, and the eyes of my understanding are continuously flooded with an abundance of light and revelation.

I am fearless. God has not given me a spirit of timidity or cowardice but of power, strength and love.

I am important. I am handsome. I am loved by the Father God.

I am courageous because God is with me.

I am free from guilt, shame, embarrassment and condemnation. My past is under the blood of Jesus. I will not allow mistakes of my past to hinder the progress of my future.

I am humble and full of love. I am not arrogant, conceited or hard-hearted.

I am free from sexual perversion of any kind. I refuse to masturbate. I refuse to watch pornography. I refuse to have sex with anyone outside of my spouse. I keep under my body.

I am redeemed from the curse of the law and every generational curse.

Tips for Remaining Pure

1. Search for an Internet filter that blocks pornography. You want to make sure that it is one where another person can monitor your Internet activity and keep you accountable.

2. Research movies before you go see them. Check the ratings and what is included in the film. Once you go through this book and clean up your gates (entry points into your life), you don't want to contaminate them again with movies or music that is full of sexual perversion.

3. If you are dating be sure to read Chapter 6 because there are several tips in there that will be helpful in maintaining purity in your dating relationship.

4. Be aware of what arouses your flesh. Each man is turned on by different things. Once you have identified these things, keep yourself away from them at all cost.

5. Avoid late night conversations on the phone, even if you feel like they are innocent and harmless. This can put your mind in an unholy head space quickly. Your mind can often wander from the topic that you are discussing.

6. If you notice something that catches your attention sexually (i.e. body parts) quickly turn away. Don't allow your flesh to take a mental screenshot because satan will bring that image back up before you in the form of a sexual fantasy. Also, plead the blood of Jesus if you do see something (see Chapter 17).

7. While you are doing normal household duties or asleep at night, put on the Word or a worship song so that your atmosphere stays infused with God. Don't always turn on the television to pass the time or help you fall asleep.

8. Make the Freedom Confessions in the back of this book every single day. Make it a part of your daily routine in the morning.

9. Avoid conversations about sex unless you are talking with your wife. We are visual beings and even casual conversations about sex can plant seeds that will later spring up.

10. Throw away anything in your house that will aid in sin, especially if you are dealing with masturbation (i.e. lotions, Vaseline, lubricants). I would rather you walk around with dry skin instead of having access to those things. Trash anything that sends you to that place.

Notes

Chapter 1

1. trigger. Dictionary.com. *Dictionary.com Unabridged.* Random House, Inc. http://dictionary.reference.com/browse/trigger (accessed: January 27, 2015).

Chapter 4

1. Rick Renner, *A Light in Darkness, Volume One: Seven Messages to the Seven Churches.* (Tulsa: Teach All Nations, 2010),143-144.

2. Ibid., 169-172.

3. James Strong. *The New Strong's Exhaustive Concordance of the Bible.* (Nashville: Thomas Nelson Publishers, 1990), 8.

Chapter 5

1. onanism. Dictionary.com. *Dictionary.com Unabridged.* Random House, Inc. http://dictionary.

reference.com/browse/onanism (accessed: January 27, 2015).

2. masturbate. Dictionary.com. *Dictionary.com Unabridged*. Random House, Inc. http://dictionary. reference.com/browse/masturbate (accessed: January 27, 2015).

3. frottage. Dictionary.com. *Dictionary.com Unabridged*. Random House, Inc. http://dictionary.reference.com/ browse/frottage (accessed: January 27, 2015).

4. Dan Savage. *Savage Love: Straight Answers From America's Most Popular Sex Columnist.* (New York: Penguin Group, 1998), 242.

5. masturbate. Dictionary.com. *Dictionary.com Unabridged*. Random House, Inc. http://dictionary. reference.com/browse/masturbate (accessed: January 27, 2015).

Chapter 9

1. pervert. Dictionary.com. *Dictionary.com Unabridged*. Random House, Inc. http://dictionary.reference.com/ browse/pervert (accessed: January 27, 2015).

Chapter 14

1. Lisa Rankin, "15 Crazy Things About Vaginas" *Psychology Today*, April 8, 2011, https://www.psychologytoday.com/blog/owning-pink/201104/15-crazy-things-about-vaginas (accessed: January 27, 2015).

Chapter 16

1. potential. Dictionary.com. *Dictionary.com Unabridged*. Random House, Inc. http://dictionary.reference.com/browse/potential (accessed: January 27, 2015).

2. submit. Dictionary.com. *Dictionary.com Unabridged*. Random House, Inc. http://dictionary.reference.com/browse/submit (accessed: January 27, 2015).

Chapter 17

1. plead. Dictionary.com. *Dictionary.com Unabridged*. Random House, Inc. http://dictionary.reference.com/browse/plead (accessed: January 27, 2015).

Chapter 18

1. choke. Dictionary.com. *Dictionary.com Unabridged.* Random House, Inc. http://dictionary.reference.com/browse/choke (accessed: January 27, 2015).

2. James Strong. *The New Strong's Exhaustive Concordance of the Bible.* (Nashville: Thomas Nelson Publishers, 1990), 68.

Chapter 20

1. distraction. Dictionary.com. *Dictionary.com Unabridged.* Random House, Inc. http://dictionary.reference.com/browse/distraction (accessed: January 27, 2015).